DEDICATION

1993, 1994 and 1995 were pivotal years in my personal life and the ministry God has given to me at North Love Baptist Church. During that time, I saw, first hand, the amazing power of Christ manifested through the transformation of Steve Curington. Brother Steve was used of the Lord to open my eyes to my responsibility and opportunity to reach into the world of addicted people and successfully help them find freedom in and through the Lord Jesus Christ. For this I am, and will forever be, eternally grateful.

Rescue and Recover is an exposition of an incredibly important sentence found in Paul's second pastoral epistle to pastor Timothy. Although I had studied this passage in prior years, 2 Timothy 2:24-26 came alive for me through my close friendship with Steve. We prayed, preached, strategized, wept, and laughed together for the final fifteen years of my brother in Christ's earthly journey, and I treasure every memory of the trip from four students in a Friday night Bible study to national and international influence, helping only God knows how many desperate men and women find the abundant life.

When Steve came back to Christ in 1993 and began to walk with the Lord reaching others for our Savior, we discussed the possibility of him leaving North Love and going off to Bible College. After much prayer, he and I knew that this was not God's will. I recall a conversation in which Brother Curington said that since it looked like he would be a layman in our church for the rest of his life,

A special thanks to the RU editorial team for tirelessly working to produce this product with us: Robert Byers, Kay Sharp, and Wendy Burks.

Cover design by Benjamin Smith
Interior Layout: Jeremy N. Jones

Reformers Unanimous Recovery Ministries

PO Box 15732, Rockford, IL 61132
Visit our website at reformerrecovery.com
Printed in Canada

Kingsbury, Paul 1953 -

Rescue and Recover

ISBN 978-0-9761498-6-6

he wanted me to know that it was his desire to be the best church member possible; and he was committed to bringing thousands of people to Christ and to North Love. Well, my brother did just that and continues to produce eternal fruit through the marvelous ministry of Reformers Unanimous International.

It is therefore, with intense gratitude to God, that I dedicate this book to Steven Boyd Curington. His life was a living epistle and a personal illustration of recovery from the snare of the devil and then becoming a servant of the Lord…rescuing and recovering multiplied others from Satan's snare.

TABLE OF CONTENTS

INTRODUCTION

In August of 1961, it was "sticky warm" in southwestern Michigan. My mother and father were listening to the crickets sing their sunset chorus and enjoying pleasant conversation with my father's parents, Grandpa and Grandma Kingsbury, outside of their cottage home in the country. Field corn stood at attention: tall, lean, and soon to be harvested. Like an army of soldiers, the tasseled sentinels surrounded Grandpop's retirement half acre on every side. A ribbon of a road and a pair of railroad tracks formed a cross in front of and to the immediate right of their house. Through my eight-year-old set of eyes, the pavement and the rails stretched to the end of the earth.

Usually, that is, twice a day, a train would rumble by. Occasionally, if my sisters and I were lucky enough to be present, those trains would stretch carefully placed pennies and our vivid imaginations. Boxcars, embossed with exotic sounding names of faraway places and containing automobiles from Detroit fascinated and entertained us as we hurriedly attempted to count the number of "cars" in the caravan before it disappeared into the horizon.

The train never stopped. Well, almost never. On a sticky, warm Saturday night in '61, a powerful locomotive and a vehicle carrying a mother and her children intersected at KL Avenue and the railroad tracks next to grandpa's house. That evening, the train did stop.

At the crossing of the road and the rails, there were no warning lights or electronic arms. No signals were present; however, there were carefully placed signs, and one could easily see and hear the approach of a train if they were paying attention. Unfortunately, that particular evening, this mother and her children somehow missed the signs, the sight, and the sound of the whistle warning them of the daily south-bound approach.

Dad told us later that an eerie silence settled over the accident scene in the moments following the initial impact of the incident and the subsequent squealing of locked up wheels and tearing sheet metal. The quiet was soon pierced, however, by the moans of people in pain.

The destroyed automobile was now in the neighboring field of corn. The driver was a young mother; and although she was injured and bleeding, she was very much awake and concerned for her children. Attempting to account for her family, she discovered that her infant child had been thrown from the vehicle and was missing. Unable to conduct a personal search due to her own needs and those of her other children, she pled for help in the rescue of her little one.

My father rescued that woman's child that night. He and others walked the aisles of corn until dad found the infant, bruised, but alive. Emergency medical personnel arrived, and an ambulance took the injured parent and her offspring to an area hospital. Eventually, though somewhat handicapped, an infant was saved and reunited with the mother. My father was a part of rescue and recovery.

My sisters and I, along with our brother who came into our home after this event, often requested that our dad tell us the story of the lost baby that he had found and returned to its mother. We enjoyed hearing about his experience, and he enjoyed telling it.

Now, many years later, I understand why this event interested us so profoundly. Each of us enjoys happy endings. Fifty years later, I find myself involved in the rescue and recovery of individuals from stubborn habits and crippling addictions; and God has graciously given me many happy endings. More than thirty-seven years of pastoral experience has provided me with a multitude of precious opportunities to be involved in the rescue of perishing souls and the recovery of spiritually broken people. This is the ministry of the New Testament church.

Second Timothy 2:24-26 gives us a three verse, one sentence summary of the mission of the servant of the Lord. This servant, along with the Lord who grants repentance, may assist in the recovery of those who are caught in the snare of the devil. The addictions program, Reformers Unanimous, is an outgrowth of this pastoral epistle admonition:

"And the servant of the Lord must not strive; but be gentle unto all men, apt to teach, patient, In meekness instructing those that oppose themselves; if God peradventure will give them repentance to the acknowledging of the truth; And that they may recover themselves out of the snare of the devil, who are taken captive by him at his will." II Timothy 2: 24 – 26

Rescuing and recovering those who are in the snare of the devil is the subject of this book. Those caught in snares need to read this exposition of these verses for their own personal benefit. They will never be unsnared without taking personal responsibility. And, for those of us who are involved in rescue and recovery, we also need this vital information for maximizing our success in helping in the rescue and recovery of others. Notice, God Himself also has a vital role in this matter, and He obviously does not need the Scriptures explained; but He has chosen to work with His servants and repentant people who are snared by Satan.

So then, as you proceed in reading *Rescue and Recover*, it is my prayer that if you are personally in the snare of the devil, you will look to God and His faithful servants for help. A Bible-believing and Bible-practicing, compassionate congregation of believers, led by a pastor who sets the example of a servant of the Lord, wants to help you. And, they can help you. If you do not know of a church such as this in your area, then contact us, and we will be glad to help you get connected.

Finally, as we begin this study, may I encourage those of you who are reading this book because someone you love is caught in the devil's snare…seek God's help to become a true servant of the Lord. There are many "happy endings" waiting for you in life as you are transformed by the Lord into effectiveness in the rescue and recovery of others.

CHAPTER ONE

THE MISSION: RESCUING THOSE ENSNARED

"And the servant of the Lord must not strive; but be gentle unto all men, apt to teach, patient, In meekness instructing those that oppose themselves; if God peradventure will give them repentance to the acknowledging of the truth; And that they may recover themselves out of the snare of the devil, who are taken captive by him at his will." (2 Timothy 2:24-26)

On December 7, 1941, the Japanese Imperial Navy launched a surprise attack on the American fleet anchored in Hawaii at Pearl Harbor. The United States was soon engaged in a horrific war. At the same time, the Japanese Army launched a massive assault on the Philippine Islands, particularly the island of Oosang. Our American soldiers and their Filipino comrades were seriously outnumbered and outgunned. Eventually, they were forced to surrender. Seventy-five thousand soldiers surrendered to the Japanese and became prisoners of war. They were taken on what is known as the Bataan Death March. More than 13,000 of those soldiers died in that arduous journey; and by the end of the war, one out of three of those taken as prisoners of war were dead. Incredible atrocities and pain and suffering were inflicted upon these men who were considered by the Japanese to be cowards for surrendering. They were looked at as sub-human by their captors. As a result, the mistreatment they endured was horrific.

In 1944, an elite group of Army Rangers under the command of Lt. Col. Henry Mucci began training in the mountains of New Guinea for a rescue mission. For almost a year, their training continued, and it was intense to say the least. One of his men later said, "I thought he was going to kills us. He called us rats; he called us everything but a child of God. I wondered why he was putting us through so much; but before it was over, there was no question about it. I knew why." Because the tide of the war had turned against Japan, the army feared that all the remaining prisoners would be murdered. In January of 1945, the 125 "Mule Skinners" as they were called joined with some Filipino guerrillas and infiltrated the POW camp at Cabanataun. They were able to rescue 513 American soldiers. These men risked their lives to rescue those held in captivity.

Paul often used the analogy of a soldier to illustrate powerful truths about the Christian life. Second Timothy 2:2-4 says, "*And the things that thou hast heard of me among many witnesses, the same commit thou to faithful men, who shall be able to teach others also. Thou therefore endure hardness, as a good soldier of Jesus Christ. No man that warreth entangleth himself with the affairs of this life; that he may please him who hath chosen him to be a soldier.*" This was not simply a statement for Timothy; this is a statement for every child of God. You may not have known this, but every Christian is conscripted into Christ's army the moment that he or she becomes a believer. Dr. John R. Rice often said, "Too many people in the army of the Lord want to be in the quartermaster corps." We are not meant to sit at ease; we are meant to be in the most difficult places, like the Mule Skinners, reaching out to rescue those held captive by the enemy. Those who have been caught in Satan's snares may either be saved or unsaved; in either case it is our responsibility to rescue them.

This mission of rescue should come as no surprise to us. If we go through the history of the church from New Testament days until now, that has been our purpose and calling. At the beginning of Christ's public ministry, when He was ready to announce the purpose for which He had come, He spoke in the synagogue of His hometown in Nazareth. Luke 4:17-18 says, ***"And there was delivered unto him the book of the prophet Esaias. And when he had opened the book, he found the place where it was written, The Spirit of the Lord is upon me because he hath anointed me to preach the gospel to the poor; he hath sent me to heal the brokenhearted, to preach deliverance to the captives, and recovering of sight to the blind, to set at liberty them that are bruised."*** The passage Jesus read is found in Isaiah 61, and He claimed it as the focus of His work here on earth—to deliver the captives.

Our culture paints an amusing picture of Satan. They costume him in a red suit with a forked tail and a pitchfork and make jokes about him. He is deadly serious about his business though. He constantly works to take people captive. If possible, he works to keep people from getting saved. In the lives of those who are saved, he works to keep them in bondage. Just as the Japanese kept their prisoners of war, Satan keeps his captives...and just as the Army Ranger Mule Skinners went to deliver the soldiers in the Philippines, we are called to deliver those who are taken captive by the devil.

For many years, our church has had the privilege of being part of the miracle of the Reformers Unanimous Addiction Ministry. We have taken seriously our responsibility to reach people with stubborn habits and addictions, both saved and unsaved alike; people who are in captivity; people who are in the snare of the devil. These are individuals who are unable to gain freedom on their own. They must have help to recover themselves out of that snare. This is a very direct response to the Scriptural mandate that the church should be on the offensive. Jesus said in Matthew 16:18, "*I will build my church; and the gates of hell shall not prevail against it.*" We are not a Christian "Elks Club"; we are soldiers in an army. There are casualties in this war, and there are prisoners who have been taken captive and are in need of rescue.

It is true that these many captives have made decisions on their own that have led them to where they are now. They may have made poor life choices, but we are not to disconnect from them. The mission of the church is for us to go and seek and rescue those who are taken captive. The snares of the enemy are manifold. They are not simply drugs. They include bitterness, unresolved conflicts, jealousy, uncontrolled anger, greed, and lust among many others. All sin is ultimately addictive. It seeks to control us. Satan brings us into his snare, and we find ourselves captive to him.

In my estimation, there has never been a day in my lifetime when there has been as many prisoners of war of the Christian faith as there is today. This is a serious and debilitating issue. Many precious men and women who have been strong soldiers for Jesus Christ, men and women whom we need at our side in fighting this great battle for our King the Lord Jesus Christ, are snared in captivity. It is a mission for the church that we help recover them out of that snare.

My goal is to explain this passage of Scripture in detail, hoping that you as an individual believer and the church where you worship and minister will become better equipped in reaching the unsaved with the wonderful message of Jesus Christ and more effective and efficient in meeting the needs of those who are ensnared—those who have been taken captive by the devil. We cannot afford to wash our hands of them or simply ignore their spiritual dilemma. We must seriously equip ourselves to reach out to them and help rescue them from their predicament. This is the mission of the New Testament Church. This is the mission of each member of the body of Christ. Consider the location of this statement given by inspiration from Paul to Timothy. There are three books in the New Testament that we call Pastoral Epistles. They are Paul's letters to Timothy in Ephesus and Titus in Crete. The location of this analogy, found in the middle of instruction to a pastor regarding his church, of soldiers rescuing captives is no accident. This, to me, is a very clear mandate from the Lord. It is a definite purpose of the church that we set out to reach people who have been caught in the snare of Satan and are in captivity to him.

Most of us have people we care deeply about who we can see are no longer victorious; and we wonder what, if anything, we can do for them. Second Timothy 2:24-26 is a summarizing instruction dealing with how we can better equip ourselves to help people recover themselves from the snares of the devil and his captivity. In order for us to be effective in this mission, **first, we must be servants of the Lord.** In verse 24, the Bible says, *"And the servant of the Lord."* This is a title that the Scripture uses for both pastors and individual believers—we are all called to be servants of the Lord. Rescuing those ensnared by the enemy is not just the responsibility of the pastor. One of the things that causes so many churches today to struggle is that only the pastor, or perhaps the pastor and a small number of people, are actively involved in serving the Lord. Those churches will always find that they have more to do than they can get done because the laborers are few.

However, this statement is more than just a description; it is also a contrast. We are to be servants of the Lord rather than servants of Satan. There are no neutral parties in this spiritual battle; you cannot be Switzerland, but you are going to have to choose sides. A person, who is ensnared themselves, is not likely to be effective at rescuing others who are ensnared. Everyone serves someone—either you serve the Lord, or you serve the devil. God has given you talents and abilities that are meant to be used to build the church and strengthen the body of Christ. If you allow yourself to be ensnared, those talents will be of no use to His Kingdom.

Continuing on in evaluating our mission, **second, we must not strive.** Verse 24 says that the servant of the Lord *"must not strive."* The word means "to go to war or quarrel, or to dispute or argue." This same word was used by Stephen in his sermon recorded in Acts chapter 7. In describing the two Hebrew men who were separated by Moses, Stephen says they were striving. They were vehemently arguing with one another. Not one person has ever been rescued from a snare by someone yelling at them. You cannot shout someone into freedom in Christ. I remember a time when my son Jason was about twenty years old, and I thought he had done something wrong. He denied it, but I'm part of the FBI—the Father's Bureau of Investigation—and I found out that indeed he had. When I confronted him, our voices started rising; and before I knew it, we were nose-to-nose. My second son, Joel, stepped between us and quietly said, "Why don't we talk a little quieter about this?"

I wasn't very thankful for his intervention at the moment, but God used Joel to calm me down. I was right and Jason was wrong about that particular situation, but the potential for ruining my relationship with my son was so real at that moment. All of the time I had invested in rearing him, all of the sermons he had heard, and everything we had taught could have been undone in a moment of anger if I had continued to strive with him. You are not going to argue someone into spiritual victory. In fact, not only does it not work, but it is actually counterproductive to your purpose to bring people back from captivity into freedom.

Continuing our intelligence briefing on what it takes to successfully rescue Satan's captives, we find that **third, we must be gentle**. Verse 24 continues that the servant of the Lord must not strive *"but be gentle to all men."* Our society has a very distorted view of what it means to be gentle. Gentleness is not weakness, nor is it exclusively a feminine trait. The same word is used in 1 Thessalonians 2:7, where Paul describes his ministry when he came to Thessalonica with the Gospel. *"But we were gentle among you, even as a nurse* *cherisheth her children.*" A mother is very careful to protect her child from danger and give him or her exactly what is needed. In the same way, we need to be considerate of the feelings and responses of those to whom we are ministering.

Earlier, I quoted one of the Rangers who was trained by Col. Mucci on the harshness of their training. After the men had learned the skills they would need for their raid, things changed. The same man said, "Once he got us trained and picked out, he loved us to death. There wasn't anything too good for us." Gentleness is strength that is under control. Just as we cannot strive with people to rescue them, we also cannot win their freedom through our abrasiveness. Some people mistakenly think that being nasty is the same as being strong. Nothing could be further from the truth.

Paul goes on to describe the successful rescue operative **fourth, as ready and willing to teach others**. Verse 24 says this servant must be *"apt to teach."* An aptitude for teaching comes from a commitment to learning. I think that every Christian should read his Bible, study his Bible, memorize his Bible, meditate on his Bible, and talk about his Bible. If you aren't sure where to start, I suggest you begin with a study of your own needs. I believe you'll find that this kind of Bible study prepares you wonderfully to minister to people who are in captivity. It's all but certain that if you work with people in captivity to sin, that you will be confronted with all kinds of questions to which you do not know the answer. If you are accustomed to learning, those questions will drive you into a deeper study of the Word of God rather than frustrating you. No one is apt to teach who has not paid the price of learning.

My goal every time I stand to teach or preach is to convey truths from God's Word to those who hear. I want to be interesting and inspiring and intellectually challenging, and I want to make people think. I want each listener to walk out better equipped to be engaged in this ministry to which God has called us as a good soldier of Jesus Christ. When we study the Word of God, we should study it from a point of view of how we can take what we have learned and teach it to others. It is said of Samuel in the Old Testament that God *"let none of his words fall to the ground."* (1 Samuel 3:19) Everything Samuel had to say was important. When I was at the airport recently, I listened in on the conversation between a two teenagers. It was like hearing a text message. They did not use complete sentences. Their words were frivolous and without benefit. My desire for my ministry is to say things that have purpose and meaning, ask questions that are relevant to spiritual life, and give direction to the lives of those who hear.

Finally, we see that to fight with the Mule Skinners to rescue captives, **we must be patient**. Often, this is the prerequisite that destroys our effectiveness. The word patience means to be cheerful while enduring something that is very difficult. My time frame on things is "now." If you ask me when I want something done, the answer isn't likely to be "later." That's how I am; but I've learned that God does not do things on my timetable. He calls me to cheerfully endure as I work with others. The devil won't give up and release his prisoners just because you show up. He's going to keep fighting to keep them ensnared, and often the process of them finding freedom will take longer than you think it should. Be patient anyhow.

Let me give you a word of warning here as well. Sometimes we endure, but we make sure that everyone knows we are not happy about it. This is not the kind of patience that helps people escape out of their snares. We may be tempted to get frustrated and give up on people when their recovery takes longer than we think it should, but God does not do that with us. Second Peter 3:9 tells us that He is "longsuffering" to us. We need to display that same character trait toward those to whom we minister.

We will be looking at many other elements of the minister of recovery as we continue on; but before we do that, I want to call your attention to the conclusion of this brief passage. In verse 26, Paul goes on to say, "*And that they may recover themselves out of the snare of the devil, who are taken captive by him at his will.*" We should do all that we can to rescue those who have been ensnared, but we cannot lose sight of the fact there is also a personal responsibility for gaining freedom. Imagine the Rangers showing up at the POW camp, having risked their lives to get there, only to have the prisoners say, "We're pretty comfortable here. We're not interested in leaving and going to freedom with you." What a tragedy that would be! Recovery is not passive; and if someone is not willing to be helped, you cannot make them receive the help you try to provide.

In January 1997, my wife, Dianne, dropped me off at church for visitation and soul winning, and then she ran to K-Mart to pick up some pictures she had taken of our son, Jason. It was dark; and when she came out of the store and opened up the car door to sit down, a man appeared from the darkness. He had a long-bladed knife, and he put it at her stomach and said, "Move over, or I'll stab you." He was trying to take her captive. At that time in Rockford, there had been a string of sexual assaults; and sadly some of those women were also killed. As Dianne moved over to the passenger side of her car, she reached up unlocked the door, opened it and jumped out. She ran across the parking lot screaming bloody murder! They never caught the man who tried to take her captive, but imagine how different things could have been if she had not taken the initiative to recover herself. I am so grateful that she was not passive in her deliverance. I would have missed out on so much joy in our lives together. I urge you not to sit back passively and hope someone comes to give you freedom. Find a church, find a pastor, or find a Christian friend who will come alongside you and work alongside to recover you. If you have a friend or loved one who is ensnared, don't give up! Patiently teach, be gentle, and continue to try to help. This is our mission, and my prayer is that this book will equip you to join God's Mule Skinners and bring freedom to the many who are enslaved by Satan today.

CHAPTER TWO

BECOMING A SERVANT OF THE LORD

"And the servant of the Lord must not strive; but be gentle unto all men, apt to teach, patient, In meekness instructing those that oppose themselves; if God peradventure will give them repentance to the acknowledging of the truth; And that they may recover themselves out of the snare of the devil, who are taken captive by him at his will." (2 Timothy 2:24-26)

In the last chapter, we looked at an overview of what it means to be involved in rescuing those who have been ensnared by the Devil. It is a great heartbreak to me to see people who once were dedicated to serving the Lord and doing His will now being held captive by Satan. In some cases, they don't even realize yet what has happened. On more than one occasion, I've tried to help someone who thinks they have found freedom by trading the "restrictions" of serving God for the allure of what Satan promises. Sometimes, I have watched a beloved comrade in arms be taken prisoner of war. Though that brings me sadness and grief, this instruction of Paul to Timothy gives me hope, because it reminds me that there is hope for those people to be recovered from their captivity. That truth makes me more determined than ever to do all that I can to rescue them.

This passage begins with a reference to "the servant of the Lord." The concept of being a servant is such a foreign one to our society, that we need to take the time to fully understand what the Spirit of God had in mind when He inspired Paul to write these words. It is hard for us to conceive how a servant could be of much value or help to anyone, but as is oftentimes true in the Bible, God's ways are not our ways. We exalt the King; God exalts the servant. We exalt those who make lots of money; and we measure their success by their bank account, by the style of their clothing, and by the possessions that they may have. Yet, the greatest who ever graced this earth, left Heaven in all of its glory and came to earth as a poor man, as a babe born in the manger, and was reared in a lower income home. He, who walked the streets of gold and sat on a throne in Heaven with angels worshiping him, having servants at His every beck and call, took the position of a servant here in this world. Our lives are forever changed because of that servant, the Lord Jesus Christ. You must never underestimate the power of a person who is willing to take the position of a servant.

When we read this phrase, *"the servant of the Lord,"* one Bible character immediately comes to mind. More than forty times, the Bible refers to Moses as "the servant of the Lord."

We know that historically, the message of Moses and his life was one of bringing about great positive change for the people of God. Here was a nation of people who had gone down to Egypt as some seventy souls; and now, after 400 years, there were millions of them in the land of Egypt. They were slaves and not guests. They were in chains and in bondage. Who would God choose to deliver them? He could have used anyone; but He chose a little slave boy, a baby who had been abandoned in the river by his own mother but raised in Pharaoh's own home and educated in all of the finest schools in Egypt, to lead the people to freedom. Moses, the servant of the Lord, rescued the entire nation of Israel from captivity.

Could it be that God could use you and me to bring people to freedom, if we are willing to become servants of the Lord also? The answer is clear from Scripture. Those who have been ensnared by Satan desperately need someone to come and help them gain their freedom. Paul had a wonderful relationship with Timothy. Paul called him his "son in the faith." First Timothy 1:2 tells us that when Paul was looking for someone to lead the church at Ephesus, a church where he had invested so much time and effort, he chose Timothy. Now, in his final letter to his protégé, Paul instructs Timothy that in order to help people in captivity, he must be more than simply the overseer or pastor of the church; he must also be a servant. Let me share some truths from Scripture with you to help you better understand what it means to be a servant of the Lord.

There are two very different concepts in the Bible that are revealed, when you study the word servant. The first corresponds to what we would call an employee today. These were people who were hired to work for someone else. Paul addresses such people in Ephesians 6:5 when we writes, *"Servants be obedient to your own masters, as unto the Lord."* The other concept of being a servant corresponds to slavery. These are people who have no freedom to determine their own course, but have it chosen for them by another. In our country's history, the issue of slavery led to the Civil War. Many of those who owned slaves were good and godly people who took the Bible descriptions of slavery and used it to justify their actions. I don't believe that is a correct interpretation of Scripture, but that is how they read it.

The Old Testament does lay out a pattern that is quite interesting to study about being a servant of the Lord. If a Hebrew man or woman was poor, he could agree to serve another for a specific number of years. There were very strict rules that governed this arrangement. Leviticus 25:39 says, *"And if thy brother that dwelleth by thee be waxen poor, and be sold unto thee; thou shalt not compel him to serve as a bondservant."* A bondservant is what we would think of as a slave. This person had no rights. He was not authorized to make decisions apart from the approval of his owner. A Jew could not compel a fellow Jew, even one in desperate financial straits to be a bondservant. Instead, Leviticus 25:40 says, *"But as an hired servant, and as a sojourner, he shall be with thee, and shall serve thee unto the year of jubilee."*

However, there was an exception to this rule. If at the end of his time of service, a servant wanted to remain with his master, then he had the opportunity to change his status. Exodus 21:5-7 says, *"And if the servant shall plainly say, I love my master, my wife, and my children; I will not go out free: Then his master shall bring him unto the judges; he shall also bring him to the door, or unto the door post; and his master shall bore his ear through with an aul; and he shall serve him forever."* A Hebrew could not be forced to become a slave, but he could choose to do so. From that time forward, he would forfeit his rights of citizenship and self-direction and be under the control of another. Why would someone make such a choice? The Bible tells us it is because of love. I'm sure you can see the connection between our status as servants (slaves) of the Lord and this Old Testament custom. Why would I give up my rights and freedom? The answer is because of love for the Master.

This was not a casual decision. Before it was made, it was carefully discussed. The rulers of the city had to be consulted to makes sure that the servant was making this choice of his own volition, rather than being forced into it by his master. If he had concerns or second thoughts, there was still time to change his mind. Once the issue was settled, they would take an awl and bore a hole in his ear. This is a very powerful symbol. From now on, the bond slave was obligated to listen to the voice of his master. He was not to choose his own way; but rather he would discern and be willing to obey the instructions given to him by his owner. Notice also that the bond slave's ear was to be pierced at the side post of the door. That meant that each time the slave entered the house, he would see a visual reminder—the mark left by the awl that had gone through his ear—that he had chosen to make a commitment to service.

When the Bible talks about the person who is effective in rescuing those who are ensnared, this is the concept—not an employee, but a slave, a "servant of the Lord." When we have fallen so in love with Jesus that we are willing to give up our rights and dedicate ourselves completely to do His will, then we are ready to bring freedom to those in captivity. Anything short of that will render us ineffective in our efforts to help people who have been caught in the snares of Satan. Our model for this role is not just found in the Old Testament, but it is also found in the New Testament as well in the life of the Lord Jesus Christ. Philippians 2:7 says of Jesus, *"But made himself of no reputation, and took upon him the form of a servant, and was made in the likeness of men."* This is not the word for an employee, but the word for slave. Jesus gave up all of His rights and privileges, all of the glory of Heaven and the worship of angelic hosts, to become a slave so that He could rescue us out of bondage from Satan. If He was willing to give up so much for us, how can we do less for the sake of those who are still prisoners to the enemy?

In John 5:30 Jesus said, *"I can of my own self can do nothing."* It sounds incredible that God would say that of Himself. *"I seek not my own will, but the will of the Father which hath sent me."* This Scripture is an example of Christ being a servant that every one of us can and should emulate. We see the same example in the believers in the early New Testament church. Though they were threatened with severe persecution and even death, they refused to stop preaching about Jesus. Why? The reason is because they had chosen to be servants of the Lord. Acts 4:29 says, *"And now, Lord, behold their threatenings: and grant unto thy servants, that with all boldness they may speak thy word."* One of the most remarkable examples of this attitude is found in the book of James. You may recall that James was a son of Joseph and Mary. Though obviously younger than the Lord Jesus Christ, James later became the pastor of the church in Jerusalem and was also used by God to write the book of James in the New Testament. He had a claim that no other Gospel writer could have made. He could have begun his epistle by calling himself James, the brother of Jesus Christ or at least James, the son of Mary, the mother of the Lord Jesus Christ. Instead, he opened his inspired letter with the words, *"James, a servant of God and of the Lord Jesus Christ."*

We looked earlier at Moses, of whom it was said forty-two times that he was "the servant of the Lord." Moses had a servant, a helper who stood with him, named Joshua. (Numbers 11:28) It's interesting that after Moses was taken to Heaven and Joshua became the leader of the people that he was known by the same title. Joshua 24:29 calls him *"Joshua, the son of Nun, the servant of the Lord."* Moses lived as an example of the servant of the Lord so much that his own servant, who was the closest person to Moses, picked up his example and also became a servant of the Lord. The fact remains, that unless we become servants of the Lord, then our ministry to others, particularly to those people who are snared by the devil, will be grossly ineffective, or it will be very, very short lived. May we never underestimate the tremendous power of someone who is simply a servant of the Lord Jesus Christ.

There was nothing particularly remarkable about the young woman named Gladys Aylward who applied to serve as a missionary with China Inland Missions. She was not very well educated and came from a poor family who lived near London, England, in the early 1900's.

Gladys was eighteen when she surrendered her life to go to China as a missionary. Because of her poor education and background, the mission board refused to send her. Instead, they asked her to serve in England to prove herself. After a few months, they told this young lady that she did not have the gifts to be a missionary. They suggested she go home, but she knew that God's call was real in her life. More than four years later, Gladys located a single missionary, a widow, in one of the mountainous provinces deep in the country of China. This older woman, Mrs. Lawson, was willing for Gladys to come and work with her in her endeavor there serving the Lord. The main means of travel those days was by ship. Gladys was so poor that she had packed all of her belonging in one little bag. She had just two pounds, nine pence (less than $10), but she knew that God was calling her to go to China.

Her trip took almost six months. When she could not get a ride from someone, Gladys walked. When she finally arrived, Gladys found the missionary, a frail old woman who was living in what had once been an inn. Things had fallen apart since the passing away of the missionary's husband, and there was no church or congregation. The inn was located at a crossroads where mule trains came through carrying goods across China to other countries. They prayed, "Lord, what can we do to get the Gospel to these people?" The older woman asked, "Gladys, what can you do?" She replied, "All that I have done was to be a servant." Mrs. Lawson said, "Well, then let's open the inn and clean the rooms. We will provide clean lodging and a place for the animals of the travelers. Then, let's endeavor to give them the Gospel."

At first, no one would come in, so Gladys, with great boldness, would go out and invite people. As the mule trains came by and the sun was setting and travelers were seeking a place of shelter and comfort, Gladys and Mrs. Lawson provided a safe place to stay overnight. Gladys would go out and grab the lead mule on several occasions by the harness and lead them back to their inn. The drivers would follow; and much to their amazement, this little inn was comfortable and very clean. Gladys and one other cook, a Chinese lady, provided delicious meals, reasonably priced. They took care of the animals and served the people. As a child, Gladys had loved to play the roles of Bible characters; so when the evening meal was finished, she and the Chinese cook would act out Bible stories for the travelers. The men loved the stories so much that they repeated them as they traveled—actually becoming couriers for the Gospel across China and the Far East. Many of those who worked on the mule trains became Christians through this simple witness.

Eventually, Mrs. Lawson died, and Gladys remained alone to keep the work going. Then, the Japanese attacked China during World War Two. Because of the hardships of war, there were many injured soldiers and many orphaned children who needed care. Gladys opened up the inn to them and met their needs as best she could. By the time the Japanese Army drew near, Gladys had more than 100 children under her care. She knew that if they stayed, they would certainly be killed. So, Gladys set out with those children, leading them on a three-month journey to safety. Gladys continued to minister to the people of China as long as her health allowed. Before she died, looking back on her life, this precious woman who was told she did not have what it took to be a missionary said, "My heart is so full of praise to my Lord Jesus, that someone so insignificant, uneducated, and ordinary in every way as myself could ever be used for His glory and the blessing of the people in China bringing them the Gospel." That's the power of being a servant of the Lord!

CHAPTER THREE
THE WAR OF WORDS THAT WILL NOT WORK

"And the servant of the Lord must not strive; but be gentle unto all men, apt to teach, patient, In meekness instructing those that oppose themselves; if God peradventure will give them repentance to the acknowledging of the truth; And that they may recover themselves out of the snare of the devil, who are taken captive by him at his will." (2 Timothy 2:24-26)

Sometimes, people say talk is cheap, but talk is not always cheap; in fact, sometimes it is very expensive. When it comes to rescuing those who are ensnared by the Devil, having the right motive is not enough to overcome using the wrong method. The Bible says in Proverbs 25:11, *"A word fitly spoken is like apples of gold in pictures of silver."* Sometimes our words are misunderstood and sometimes they are destructive, but it is imperative that we guard our words as we communicate with those who are in captivity. Paul is inspired here by the Spirit of God to warn Timothy against striving—arguing rather than aiding. Let me share some wise words with you regarding the matter of our speech.

Will Rogers once said, "Never miss a good chance to shut up." Earl Wilson said, "If you wouldn't write it and sign it, don't say it." Someone else said, "Of those that say nothing, few are silent." Winston Churchill said, "By swallowing words unsaid, no one has ever harmed the stomach." Edward Allen Poe said, "The true genius shudders at incompleteness and usually prefers silence to saying something that is not everything it should be." Ann Landers said, "The problem with talking too fast is that you may say something that you haven't thought of yet." Another said, "The easiest way to save face is to keep the lower half shut." And a wise individual added, "Even a fish wouldn't get into trouble if he kept his mouth shut."

Abraham Lincoln said, "It is better to keep one's mouth shut and be thought a fool, than to open it and remove all doubt." A Chinese proverb says, "Not the fastest horse can catch a word said in anger." Someone said, "Discussion is an exchange of knowledge. Argument is an exchange of ignorance." Yet another said, "I wish my mouth had a backspace key." George Bernard Shaw said concerning a particular woman, "The trouble with her is that she lacks the power of conversation but not the power of speech." Austin O'Malley said, "If you keep your mouth shut you will never put your foot in it." Someone once said, "Talk is cheap because the supply usually exceeds demand." And to that a wise man added, "When you are arguing with a fool make sure that he isn't doing the same thing."

Words are not meant to be used as weapons of war, but often they are. When the Bible speaks of us not striving, it is telling us not to go to war with our words. We will never reach people by striving with them. The word strive, according to the Strong's Exhaustive

Concordance of the Bible, literally means "to go to war, to quarrel, to dispute, to fight, to argue." Let's look at some other places in Scripture where this same word is used to help us understand better the instruction for those who would be at work rescuing those ensnared.

John 6:52 says, *"The Jews therefore strove among themselves, saying, How can this man give us his flesh to eat?"* The teaching of Jesus so confused the Jews who were listening, that they actually began arguing over what He meant. Jesus did not allow Himself to be drawn into their arguments. Actually, that is part of a Messianic prophecy recorded Isaiah 42:1-4 and quoted in Matthew 12:18&19, *"Behold my servant, whom I have chosen; my beloved, in whom my soul is well pleased: I will put my spirit upon him, and he shall shew judgment to the Gentiles. He shall not strive, nor cry; neither shall any man hear his voice in the streets."* If Jesus is our example in everything, including the ministry of rescuing those ensnared by Satan, then it follows that we must not allow ourselves to be dragged into futile arguments with those we are trying to help.

When we cross the line from conversing about a subject to arguing about it, then that can lead to broken relationships, insecurity, and resentment. Nothing glorifying to God or beneficial for others is ever accomplished by our arguing. This warning against striving is not a call to inaction; but rather, it is a call to proper action. Arguing can be damaging. Many of those who are being held prisoner do not even recognize it. Many of them are very comfortable in their snare. Using our words as weapons of war will never work. Listen to these warnings from Scripture. Titus 3:9 says, *"But avoid foolish questions, and genealogies, and contentions, and strivings about the law;* *for they are unprofitable and vain."* As remarkable as it may seem, people can actually get into arguments and fights over the Bible. Second Timothy 2:14 says, *"Of these things put them in remembrance,* *charging them before the Lord that they strive not about words to no* *profit, but to the subverting of the hearers."* Rather than drawing a person closer to the Lord, victory, and recovery, our argumentative words are likely to subvert the cause and drive those we are trying to reach further away.

Striving can lead to violent behavior. Look at Exodus 21:18, 19 & 22 for example, *"And if men strive together, and one smite another* *with a stone, or with his fist, and he die not, but keepeth his bed: If he* *rise again, and walk abroad upon his staff, then shall he that smote him* *be quit: only he shall pay for the loss of his time, and shall cause him* *to be thoroughly healed. If men strive, and hurt a woman with child,* *so that her fruit depart from her and yet no mischief follow: he shall be* *surely punished, according as the woman's husband will lay upon him:* *and he shall pay as the judges determine."* It is interesting to note that most violence in our culture today is domestic violence. In fact, more than 50% of the murders in the United States of America are family related. Often, a war of words is what leads to physical violence. In the heat of an argument, we lose all sensibility. We lose our ability to converse intelligently and in a God-honoring way.

Striving not only leads to violence, but it can lead to vulgarity as well. Leviticus 24:10-14 says, *"And the son of an Israelitish woman,* *whose father was an Egyptian, went out among the children of Israel:* *and this son of the Israelitish woman and a man of Israel strove together* in the camp; And the Israelitish woman's son blasphemed the name of the LORD, and cursed. And they brought him unto Moses: (and his mother's name was Shelomith, the daughter of Dibri, of the tribe of Dan:) And they put him in ward, that the mind of the LORD might be shewed them. And the LORD spake unto Moses, saying, Bring forth him that hath cursed without the camp; and let all that heard him lay their hands upon his head, and let all the congregation stone him."

In the middle of their striving, this man lost his temper and blasphemed the very name of God. I don't know how many times I have been working with a married couple, and one of them (usually the wife) will say something like, "I can't believe he talked to me that way." Striving tempts us to use wrong language, both about God and toward others.

Striving creates a breach in our relationship with the Lord as well. Numbers 26 describes the rebellion of Korah and some of the leaders of the people against Moses. These men launched a vicious attack on the leaders God had chosen for His people (That's always a bad idea!), and God came to their defense. What I want you to see if that they thought they were striving against Moses and Aaron, but God saw it differently. Numbers 26:9 says, *"And the sons of Eliab; Nemuel, and Dathan, and Abiram. This is that Dathan and Abiram, which were famous in the congregation, who strove against Moses and against Aaron in the company of Korah, when they strove against the LORD."* You may say that your problem is just with others; but if you are striving with Christians, particularly with leaders, then you have a problem with God. If you know the rest of that story, God opened the ground and Korah and those who followed him were killed for their rebellion.

The reality is that sometimes we get our hearts in such bad shape that we actually fight against God, and no man ever has the right to argue with Him. Isaiah 45:9 says, *"Woe unto him that striveth with his Maker!"* Isaiah 41:11 says, *"They that strive with thee shall perish."* If God is speaking to your heart through hearing preaching, teaching, or your own study of the Word, then you had better listen. In his poem, *The Prodigal Son,* James Weldon Johnson wrote, "Young man, young man, your arm's too short to box with God." That is a fight which can only lead to your own destruction.

With this Bible background in mind, let's return to striving specifically as it relates to helping those who are ensnared. The person you are trying to help may be wrong, and your intention may be solely to help them. Despite that, verbally attacking them and arguing with them will not produce a good result. By doing so, you are demonstrating a lack of trust in God and God's ability to move that person in the right direction. God does not need you to argue with them; God is very capable of arguing with them Himself, and He is perfect at it. When we enter into an argument, our own hypocrisy becomes evident. The person you want to help may say, "How dare you talk to me as if I'm wrong? What about you?" The argument escalates. You may say, "I would never say anything wrong, I just love that person so much and want to help them." However, if you get in the wrong circumstances, you can say things that are absolutely abominable. I don't care how good of a Christian you are or how long you have been saved. We can revert back to that kind of behavior very, very rapidly.

I heard a story about a preacher who decided to take a walk around the block on a sunny day. As he went down the street, he saw one of the neighborhood boys washing a lawnmower, so he stopped to ask him what he was doing. The boy replied, "Preacher, I am washing the lawnmower so I can sell it." The preacher needed a lawnmower, so he asked, "How much do you want for it?" The boy answered, "Just enough to buy a bicycle." The preacher had a bicycle hanging in his garage that he never used, so he said, "I have a bicycle. Do you want to trade me the lawnmower for the bike" The boy asked to look at it; and after he saw that it was a nice bike, he said, "We have a deal." Happily, he got on the bike and rode away. The preacher decided to go ahead and cut the grass since he now had a lawnmower. He went inside and changed clothes, and then tried to start the lawnmower. He checked the gas and oil in the lawnmower, primed it, and pulled the cord. Nothing happened. He pulled it again and again, but it still wouldn't start. About that time, the boy went riding past on his new bike. The preacher called out, "Hey kid, this lawnmower that you traded me does not work." The boy said, "It does work, but I forgot to tell you that you have to curse at it to get it started." The preacher said "Son, I'm a man of God. I don't even remember how to curse." The little boy said as he was riding away, "Keep pulling that cord, Mister, and it will come back to you." If you start striving, there is no telling what may eventually come out of your mouth!

However, there is another kind of striving—not arguing, but working earnestly—that we should adopt. We see this word used in Romans 15:20 where Paul wrote, *"Yea, so have I strived to preach the gospel."* This kind of striving is one we do together; not a strife between two people but a partnership between them. Philippians

1:27 says, "*Only let your conversation be as it becometh the gospel of Christ: that whether I come and see you, or else be absent, I may hear of your affairs, that ye stand fast in one spirit, with one mind striving together for the sake of the gospel, we ought to strive together for the faith.*" There is a world of difference between the two approaches. Working together toward a common goal may result in someone coming out of the snare and returning back to a place of usefulness for God, while arguing is sure to drive them away. It is vitally important that we hold ourselves accountable in our words in order to overcome the natural tendency to be argumentative and abusive and thus detrimental to the cause of Christ.

CHAPTER FOUR

CONVERSING WITHOUT ARGUING

"And the servant of the Lord must not strive; but be gentle unto all men, apt to teach, patient, In meekness instructing those that oppose themselves; if God peradventure will give them repentance to the acknowledging of the truth; And that they may recover themselves out of the snare of the devil, who are taken captive by him at his will." (2 Timothy 2:24-26)

It is easy to say that the servant of the Lord must not strive, must not argue, must not fight, and must not go to war with people. We can understand both from Scripture and from our own experiences that no one is moved and motivated to recover themselves out of the snare of the devil by the clever arguments of any human being. We have seen from God's Word in many, many places that it is not our abilities and clever words; it is not our convincing arguments that lead people to Christ for salvation or for sanctification. The question then is, how do we help people recover themselves out of the snares of Satan, which is likely to involve an element of confrontation without becoming argumentative? These conversations, by their very nature, are going to be difficult to navigate. The fact that they are difficult does not give us a pass—we are still supposed to working to deliver these people. So, how can we confront and converse without arguing? There are three principals that I have discovered in the Bible concerning this matter that if followed will maximize the possibility of someone responding properly and recovering themselves from captivity.

First, **recognize that words have the power of life and death**. Proverbs 18:21 says, *"Death and life are in the power of the tongue."* This is not a figurative or poetic statement; it is literally true. We see this principle illustrated at the very beginning of the Bible. Genesis chapter 1 records the creation of the world as God spoke things into existence out of nothing. God's words are powerful words. God's words bring life. As He spoke, not only were various plants, animals, and man created, but they were given the ability to continue that life by reproducing after their kind. Yet, we see another speaker in Genesis 3. The serpent came and spoke to Eve and called the words of God into question. Satan's words bring death. Every word that you and I speak ultimately has its origins in either God or in the Devil. There is no neutrality in our words; there are simply no casual words. They may be casual to you and me, but life and death are in the power of the tongue. Every word that you and I speak lends itself to life and leads those to whom we are speaking toward right, or it lends itself to death and will lead them toward what is wrong.

Recognizing this truth is foundational to having conversations that do not lead to arguments. When we realize the vital importance of our words, it helps us put a guard over our tongue. We should stop, consider, and weigh carefully that which we plan to say before we speak it. I suggest you consider taking the time to write out those things that you are going to say in a conversation that you know could lead to an argument. For example, if you are about to talk to a rebellious child, that is a conversation fraught with possibilities for emotional turmoil. Rather than just diving in, sit down and identify the specific issues that need to be dealt with, and then stick to your list. Beyond that, be sure you are in control of your own emotions before you begin the conversation. If you start out angry or frustrated, it is likely both of you will be angry and frustrated before you are done talking. Many times, our failure to keep conversation going in the right direction is a result of not thinking before we speak.

Some years ago, I knew a man who came to Christ and began to grow dynamically and very rapidly as a believer. He was very generous toward God's work. He was a layman, but he found ways to become involved in the work of the ministry. He traveled to mission fields to help encourage missionaries. But, on one missions trip he got involved in a dispute between some preachers and some missionaries. Some bad things were said, and some things were done that should not have been done, and it discouraged him. When he came back from that trip, his spiritual condition changed. Should he have done right and kept going? Yes. But, there was death in some of the words that were said to him, and it brought him to a place where the enemy could ensnare him. As our children sing in Sunday school, "Be careful little tongue what you say."

Second, **remember that words proceed out of the heart**. If you are going to speak life-giving words to others, your heart is going to have to be a source that is pure, right, wholesome, and good.

In talking to the Pharisees, Jesus said, *"O generation of vipers, how can ye, being evil, speak good things? For out of the abundance of the heart the mouth speaketh. A good man out of the good treasure of the heart bringeth forth good things: and an evil man out of the evil treasure bringeth forth evil things. But I say unto you, that every idle word that men shall speak, they shall give account thereof in the day of judgment. For by thy words thou shalt be justified, and by thy words thou shalt be condemned."* (Matthew 12:34-37) So often we say something harsh, cutting, or unkind and then say, "I didn't mean that. That's not what I really think." When we do that, we are not telling the truth. What we should say instead is, "I'm sorry for the sinful attitude in my heart that led me to say that." Proverbs 30:5 declares that every word of God is pure, and that is true because God Himself is pure. His heart is pure, thus His words are pure. An impure heart will always produce impure words. Jesus often called the Pharisees hypocrites because it is possible for someone to use proper words with an improper motive. Speaking rightly is not simply saying the right thing; it is also saying the right thing from a pure heart, with pure motives.

Words that tend to death are a powerful indicator that there is a problem in our heart. James put it this way in his epistle in the famous passage on the tongue. *"For every kind of beasts, and of birds, and of serpents, and of things in the sea, is tamed, and hath been tamed of mankind: But the tongue can no man tame; it is an unruly evil, full of deadly poison. Therewith bless we God, even the Father; and therewith curse we men, which are made after the similitude of God. Out of the same mouth proceedeth blessing and cursing. My brethren, these things ought not so to be. Doth a fountain send forth at the same place sweet* water and bitter? Can the fig tree, my brethren, bear olive berries? either a vine, figs? So can no fountain both yield salt water and fresh? Who is a wise man and endued with knowledge among you? Let him shew out of a good conversation his works with meekness of wisdom. But if ye have bitter envying and strife in your hearts, glory not, and lie not against the truth."* (James 3:7-14) What James is reminding us is that our words proceed out of our hearts. The reason we curse others, the reason we speak words of death instead of words of life, is not that we choose the wrong words, but that we have a wrong heart.

Before you try to rescue someone else from the snares of the Devil, take care that your own heart has not been polluted by sin. The key to effectively communicating words of life that will motivate someone to make positive changes is found in the heart of the speaker. Pure words bring life, but pure words cannot come out of an impure heart. James further tells us that an evil heart cannot remain concealed for long. James 4:1&2 says, *"From whence come wars and fightings among you? come they not hence, even of your lusts that war in your members? Ye lust, and have not: ye kill, and desire to have, and cannot obtain: ye fight and war, yet ye have not, because ye ask not."* Why is there so much tension, dissension, and even outright fighting among the people of God? It comes from problems in the heart. When your heart is filled with envy and lust, there will not be peace in your life. No wonder David said, *"Let the words of my mouth and the meditations of my heart, be acceptable in thy sight O Lord."* (Psalm 19:14) It is not simply a matter of pure words; it is a matter of having a pure heart. When our hearts are pure, our words will be pure.

Finally, **we must trust God for the power to take the pure**

words that come from our pure heart and use them to bring life. I have a responsibility to speak, but God is the one who changes hearts and lives. God is the one who brings deliverance. That is not my job, and the words that I speak need to be spoken in faith. My wisdom, my insight, my persuasiveness is not enough to get the job done. Ephesians 6:17 tells us to take *"the sword of the Spirit, which is the word of God."* When I give people God's Word, I am giving them input that He has promised to bless. If I am focused on changing the person and trying to do it myself, and it doesn't happen immediately; then I am at risk of falling into the trap of arguing and striving with them. If instead, I am trusting God, then I can wait for the results even if I don't see them at first.

Every Saturday morning, several of the men of our church gather together in the auditorium, and we pray for the church. One of the things that we pray for is for the power of the Spirit of God on our services. Why do we pray for that? We pray for God's power because, as the old hymn says, "All is vain unless the Spirit of the Holy One comes down." I study and prepare and plan a message to speak to the needs of those who come—that's not enough. We sing songs that are doctrinally correct and uplifting—that's not enough. No matter how right we are in our practice, we must have God's power or no lasting results will be achieved. Even if our words are life-giving words from a pure heart, without the power of God's Spirit, they will not free anyone from the snares of Satan.

Paul knew this truth well. When he reflected back on the beginning of his ministry at Corinth he said, *"And I, brethren, when I came to you, came not with excellency of speech or of wisdom."* (1

Corinthians 2:1) Paul was an extremely well-educated man. He spoke many languages and had studied at the feet of Gamaliel. That would be the equivalent of an Ivy League education today. Paul did not try to impress the people of Corinth with his brilliance by ministering in a Greek culture that admired philosophers like Plato, Aristotle, and Socrates. Instead, he says, *"And I was with you in weakness, and in fear, and in much trembling. And my speech and my preaching was not with enticing words of man's wisdom, but in demonstration of the Spirit and of power."* (1 Corinthians 2:3)

Some of the most profound times in my life when God moved in my heart, bringing me under deep conviction, bringing me to a place of renewed dedication and revival, and calling me to surrender and acknowledge a sin in my life, were during sermons I cannot even remember today.

I don't mean to downplay the minister of the preachers who not doubt planned and worked and prayed over those messages, I am simply saying that it was the Spirit of God using them in my heart and life to change me for the better. Sometimes, we trust in our own abilities rather than relying on Him. We think that if we can just talk the person into doing the right thing or find the right way to tell them what they need to do, we can make it happen. I can tell you right now that you are not going to be able to do it. Instead, seek to have a pure heart and to speak the truth to the person you wish to help out of a pure heart using the pure words of God and having a biblical basis for everything you say and present to them. Then, through the power of the Spirit of God, your words can be life changing!

The first two sermons I preached as a teenager demonstrated

this truth to me so clearly. The first time I preached was at a rescue mission. I very meticulously prepared a sermon on the second coming of Christ. I had copious notes on the second coming of Christ taken from the texts in First Corinthians 15 and First Thessalonians. Calling it a disaster would be too kind. No one got anything out of it. While I was preaching, a drunken lady stood up and cursed at me. She said, "Sit down and shut up so we can go to dinner!" I finally gave up and quit. I was totally humiliated. I never wanted to preach again. Thank God that the man who worked with the teens at our church, Rex DuVall said, "You're preaching next week at the jail." I thought he was joking. I hoped he was joking. If I could not handle the rescue mission, how could I handle a jail? I said, "I'm not going to do that." He said, "Yes, you are." I said, "No, I'm not." He went by and had a word with my father. My dad said, "Yes, you are." And I did. Before that second sermon, Brother DuVall gave me some of the best advice I have ever received. He said, "Don't try to impress people with how much you know about the Bible. Ask God to give you message from His Word and then share the message with these men from your heart, asking God to bless it."

I was anything but confident when I stood to speak. All the members of my "congregation" were wearing suits—orange jumpsuits. And sure enough, not long after I started preaching, I was interrupted again. But, not everything was the same. A man stood up and said, "Mister, I want to get saved." Then, another man said, "I would like to do that too." I did not get to finish either of the sermons, but the results were very different. When I relied on God and He worked, lives were changed. Before you approach someone to try to help them escape from the captivity of the enemy, seek the power of God. That changes the impact of everything you say and can actually bring them to freedom.

CHAPTER FIVE

A GENTLE MAN

"And the servant of the Lord must not strive; but be gentle unto all men, apt to teach, patient, In meekness instructing those that oppose themselves; if God peradventure will give them repentance to the acknowledging of the truth; And that they may recover themselves out of the snare of the devil, who are taken captive by him at his will." (2 Timothy 2:24-26)

Recently, a would-be shoplifter was spotted by video surveillance in a Best Buy store in Augusta, Georgia, as he attempted to steal a laptop computer. He was leaving the store with the computer concealed inside his coat when he was confronted by security personnel. Rather than surrender, he pulled out a knife and threatened the guards before running out of the store. Sadly for him, four United States Marines were outside the store collecting for the "Toys for Tots" drive to provide presents for needy children. Recognizing what was going on, they stepped in to stop the thief. According to the news report, one of the Marines suffered a minor stab wound to his shoulder. The hapless shoplifter was transported to a local hospital with two broken arms, a broken leg, several broken ribs, a broken jaw, a broken nose, and multiple lacerations. According to the police report, he suffered those injuries in a fall as he attempted to escape!

There is a time and a place for physical force, but there is also a time for restraint. One of those times is when we are dealing with someone who has been ensnared by Satan. Dealing with such people can be very frustrating, because often they are not fully aware the danger of their situation. They may feel completely at ease and free, though they are ensnared. Satan is a master deceiver. In fact, in verse 25, Paul describes their need of God granting "them repentance to the acknowledging of the truth." No one ever changes the way he lives, until he first changes the way he thinks. However, that is normally a process that takes quite a bit of time. If we do not guard our hearts when dealing with someone who doesn't realize his desperate need for help, it can create a lot of frustration and even anger on our part as they refuse our offers to help. The instruction that we see here to be gentle with those in captivity is crucial.

When we think of gentleness, we often focus on good manners or proper etiquette. During the presidency of Abraham Lincoln, reportedly, there was a meeting of government leaders, and Lincoln was a part of the conversation. One of the men walked up, looked around and said, "Since I see there are no ladies present, I want to tell you a humorous story." The president stopped him and said, "Excuse me, there may be no ladies present, but there are gentlemen." While good matters are important, the Bible is not speaking of being a gentle man or gentle woman in that sense. Gentleness, biblically speaking, deals with the proper control of our hands—that we do not use them to strike at others. Rescuing people from the captivity of the Devil requires that we remain in control of ourselves physically as well as emotionally. In Titus 3, Paul gives us a good sense of the gentle person from a biblical standpoint. Titus 3:2 says, *"To speak evil of no man, to be no brawlers, but gentle."* The contrast is drawn between a brawler and a person who is gentle. When we think of brawling, we think of something like a barroom brawl, but not all physical abuse takes place inside a tavern; it can be found in other places as well. There was a story in the news of the fight in a Baptist church in Alabama where a deacon pulled a knife and stabbed one staff member and the music minister used a Taser on the pastor.

I wish I didn't have to say this, but there are people in the church who are not gentle. One of the greatest shocks I have had in the ministry was irrefutable evidence that a man I deeply loved and highly respected as a minister of the Gospel of Jesus Christ was horribly abusing his teenage daughter. This man and his wife isolated her from everyone, even putting paper over the windows of their home to hide what was going on behind their closed doors. Today, both that preacher and his wife are in prison, and they will likely remain there for the rest of their lives. That is a tragedy; and though there are other contributing factors, it is partly tied to a lack of gentleness. In First Thessalonians, the Apostle Paul reviews his method of ministry when he arrived in Thessalonica. Though he was ministering and witnessing to people from a pagan background with an immoral philosophy of life, he said, *"But we were gentle among you, even as a nurse cherisheth her children."* (1 Thessalonians 2:7)

In effect, Paul was saying, "We didn't come to Thessalonica and endeavor to win you to Christ and then to obedience to the Lord by beating you into it. We didn't use our voices to demean you and tear you apart. We didn't physically grab you and shake you. Instead, we were gentle when we were with you. In fact, we were so careful in our dealings with you, it was as if we were nursing little infant children; that is how cautious and careful we were with our words and our actions." Where did Paul get that pattern of ministry? After all, he had once been a brawler, persecuting the church and dragging men and women before the judges to be condemned to death for being Christians. In being gentle, Paul was following the example of Christ. In Second Corinthians 10:1 he wrote, *"Now I, Paul myself beseech you by the meekness and gentleness of Christ, who in presence am base among you, but being absent am bold toward you."* As in everything, Jesus is the perfect pattern for us to follow in gentle ministry to those in bondage to Satan.

There is another powerful example of the Bible concept of gentleness as the avoidance of physical mistreatment of others in the Old Testament. During the rebellion by Absalom against his father, David fled from the city of Jerusalem. His army was preparing to face the soldiers who were following Absalom, and David gave instructions to the three commanding generals over his forces regarding their treatment of his son. Second Samuel 18:5 says, *"And the king commanded Joab and Abishai and Ittai, saying, Deal gently for my sake with the young man, even with Absalom. And all the people heard when the king gave all the captains charge concerning Absalom."* The battle was fought in a dense forest. In fact, the Scripture says that the difficult terrain resulted in the death of more men than the battle did. During the battle, Absalom was riding on a mule, and his long hair became tangled in the branches of an oak tree. The mule ran off, leaving him hanging in mid-air, suspended by his hair. Of course, you know the story. When Joab found out that Absalom was helpless, he went and killed him in direct violation of David's order. He did not deal with him gently. The Bible concept of gentleness is not simply talking soft words; it is how we physically deal with people. Hands are not for hurting those we love. So, we see that the Bible not only warns against wrong words (striving) but wrong actions (gentleness) as well.

David gives us another beautiful picture of gentleness in Psalm 18. Bible scholars believe that this is one of the last of David's Psalms, written near the end of his life. David had been in constant battles since the time he was young. He fought Goliath when he was still a teenager, then he went into Saul's army and fought the Philistines. After that, he had to run from Saul; and then once he became king, the wars continued. Finally, late in his life, he fought another group of giants. It is interesting to me that David's first battle and his last battle were against giants. Sometimes, we make the mistake of thinking that because we have won a few battles things are going to get easier. That is not the way it works. As we grow and mature in the Lord, the battles become greater. We would like to think that we have fought our biggest battles in our youth, but David fought his biggest battles in his older years. You may think that it's going to get easier and easier as you get older, but that is absolutely wrong. Now that the battles are finished, David reflects back on his relationship with God and what God has done for him. Psalms 18:35 says, *"Thou hast also given me the shield of thy salvation: and thy right hand hath holden me up, and thy gentleness hath made me great."*

Notice the link that David makes here between God's hand and His gentleness. The hands of God are mentioned over and over again in Scripture. God uses His hands to help people, to hold them up, to encourage, and strengthen them. Hands are not for hurting people; hands are for helping people. I heard evangelist John Bishop preach and give his testimony. He was stricken with aseptic meningitis, and his mind reverted all the way back to his infancy. He forgot everything he had learned. He had to go back and relearn his ABCs, his colors, how to count, and all the other things we learn as children. One of the things he talked about in describing his experience was the importance of touch. Touch is more than just a part of the way we communicate; touch is a vital part of wellness and good health. If you study the Gospel, you will find that many of the miracles of Jesus involved Him touching someone. He didn't have to do that—His words alone could heal any illness. But the people to whom He ministered needed that touch. It was important and meaningful to them. The Bible tells us that mothers would bring their little children to Jesus so He could touch them.

When I've taught on this, some people have asked, "What about discipline?" That's a good question and an important issue. In the Bible, you will not find the hand ever suggested as an instrument for the discipline of children. The Bible is not against physical punishment; the Bible says to use "a rod." The correction of children at times does need to involve physical punishment, but that physical punishment should not be done with the hand. The hand is to be associated with help and healing rather than being associated with pain and punishment. I don't know what kind of training my parents had on the topic of discipline, but they followed this pattern. My father spanked me with his belt. In the winter, my mother would use a wooden spoon; the rest of the year, she used a willow switch from the tree outside our home. (If I was going to get punished, I hoped it was in the winter. Those switches hurt!) There was one time when my father used his hand to punish me. Later, he came and asked my forgiveness. He confessed that he had crossed a line. I don't remember the spankings I got; but more than forty years later, I do remember that particular day. My father never had to discipline me again the rest of the time I lived in his home. The hand is meant to bring help, not hurt.

We also find the concept of gentle hands in the words of the prophet Isaiah. He paints a beautiful picture of God's concern and care for us using the analogy of a shepherd with his sheep. Isaiah 40:11 says, *"He shall feed his flock like a shepherd: he shall gather the lambs with his arm, and carry them in his bosom, and shall gently lead those that are with young."* There is a temptation when we're leading someone to freedom to lead harshly. We may try to pull them along. After all, we know where they need to be, and it's frustrating that they won't hurry up and get there. In contrast, God leads us gently with His hands; and that is the way we should treat those who are ensnared. At a church where I was preaching not too long ago, I met a young couple who had recently been saved. Though they were a wonderful couple, they asked to talk to me about a challenge they were facing in their marriage. The wife was very much afraid of her husband touching her. Of course, you can imagine the problem that creates. She said, "I cringe when he even lifts his hand to caress my face." I asked her why she responded that way. She said, "When I was a child, my parents used their hands to strike me. When they lifted their hands, it was just slap me, to smack me, or to hit me." She was a married adult woman, but it was very hard for her to overcome a pattern that was established when she was abused as a child. What message are your hands sending to the people in your life?

CHAPTER SIX

HOW TO HANDLE YOUR HANDS

"And the servant of the Lord must not strive; but be gentle unto all men, apt to teach, patient, In meekness instructing those that oppose themselves; if God peradventure will give them repentance to the acknowledging of the truth; And that they may recover themselves out of the snare of the devil, who are taken captive by him at his will." (2 Timothy 2:24-26)

I n the last chapter, we defined a gentle person as not simply someone who has good manners, and is conscientious and kind. We saw from Scripture that gentleness means not physically attempting to solve problems through using our hands abusively. As hard as it is for me to believe, it is estimated that nearly four million children under the age of twelve will be physically abused this year. Even worse, more than 2,000 children died last year because they were murdered by a family member or someone who lived in the home. Eighty per cent of childhood fatalities are due to abuse. More children will die from child abuse this year in our country than from accidental falls, choking on food, suffocation, and house fires combined. We are a nation of violent people. Where does that violence arise? How can we grapple with the tendency to respond violently to problems? To answer those questions, we need to look at the Bible to find the contributing factors that lead to violence.

The first cause of violence is pride. Proverbs 13:10 says, *"Only by pride cometh contention."* We see this illustrated in the story of Cain and Abel in Genesis chapter 4. It is not surprising that a war of words often escalates into acts of violence. It springs from the pride that so easily finds root deep within in our hearts. If our feelings are hurt, or we don't get what we think we deserve, or someone else gets something we think should have come to us, why are we angry? The only reason is because of pride.

"And Adam knew Eve his wife; and she conceived, and bare Cain, and said, I have gotten a man from the LORD. And she again bare his brother Abel. And Abel was a keeper of sheep, but Cain was a tiller of the ground. And in process of time it came to pass, that Cain brought of the fruit of the ground an offering unto the LORD. And Abel, he also brought of the firstlings of his flock and of the fat thereof. And the LORD had respect unto Abel and to his offering, But unto Cain and to his offering he had not respect." (Genesis 4:1-5)

God responded very differently to the offerings of Cain and Abel. He "had respect" to Abel, not to Cain. Abel was obedient; Cain was not. Abel was right, not just in his sacrifice, but in his heart. Yet, when God reproved Cain, rather than repenting, he became angry. God's rebuke struck a chord of pride in Cain. Innate within the human soul is a personal desire to be accepted, to be admired, and to be appreciated. We love to be complemented. There is nothing wrong with wanting to be accepted by God, but there is something wrong with blaming someone else if we are not. God does not make mistakes. He only holds us responsible for what we have done or failed to do. It is never someone else's fault if I do wrong. Yet, how many times do we respond as Cain did? The Bible says he was wroth (angry) and his countenance fell. His inward feelings showed on his face. Then, they came out in his actions. Genesis 4:8 says, *"And Cain talked with Abel his brother: and it came to pass, when they were in the field, that Cain rose up against Abel his brother, and slew him."*

This awful act of violence, the first murder in the history of the world, arose directly from the pride in Cain's heart. Abel did nothing wrong. Adam and Even did nothing wrong. God, of course, did nothing wrong. The only one who did wrong was Cain, and he then compounded the problem because of his pride. It's natural for us to want to be respected; but because of our sin nature, it is also natural for us to respond with violence when we feel that we are not being respected. The desire for respect gone awry leads to pride, and pride is a horrible thing. His conversation with God should have humbled Cain. He should have said, "You are right; I am wrong. I am sorry for bringing the wrong offering. I am sorry for my rebellion. Will You please forgive me and let me bring You the right offering?" He would have gained the respect of God, because there is great honor and blessing in humbling ourselves before Him. Humble pie tastes awful. None of us like to eat it. But we refuse to eat humble pie, when our pride leads us to anger instead of allowing us to repent; we are treading on dangerous ground indeed.

In 1973, I was invited to serve as a summer intern at my home church. The pastor I had grown up under was gone, and a new pastor had come. I had two years of Bible college under my belt, and I knew it all. The pastor and I had different opinions about a lot of things. One Sunday, he was going to be out of town, and he asked me to preach. He said, "I want you to show me your sermon before I leave—not just the outline. I want to see the whole thing. I prepared the sermon and gave it to him. He told me there were a few hot buttons that he did not want me to talk about, and he identified them. Well you can imagine how I responded to that! As soon as he got out of town, I threw away that sermon and wrote another one. I was going to set that church straight with just one message. It was going to be the second coming of Jonathan Edwards and his famous sermon "Sinners in the Hands of an Angry God." (I didn't know back then that he got fired by his church!) Somehow, I convinced myself that it wasn't going to be a problem—that the pastor wouldn't find out, or that things would go so well that he wouldn't be mad. He did find out, and he was mad. I would like to be able to tell you that I repented, but I didn't. My pride rose up, and I defended my actions. Then, I went to look for somewhere else to serve.

I was in Rockford when Bill Gothard came to town. He had a very conservative program in those days, and I went to hear him. It seemed like everything he said was pointed directly at me. That little man in the blue suit was stepping all over my toes. He said, "Kingsbury, you rotten scoundrel, you undermined the authority of the pastor." I felt miserable. I thought, *what should I do?* About that time, he told me, "You need to go see him." *When should I do that,* I thought? He answered that one too. "You should do it as soon as possible." Well, I was planning to go home for Christmas, so I thought that I would look him up then. Not long after I got home, someone drove up and knocked on the door. As far as I know my pastor had never visited my parents' house before. I saw him get out of the car, and I went to answer the door. I said, "Dad, it's for me." He said, "I don't think anyone knows you are here." "That's probably true, but it's for me." I stood that at the front door and I said, "I apologize for what I did. I'm so sorry. Would you please forgive me?" He said, "Yes I will. You're right—what you did was rotten!" Part of me had been hoping that he would say, "I was wrong too." I wanted him to say that in the worst way. He didn't.

I was just on my third or fourth bite of humble pie and the pride was starting to come back. I could feel my tongue getting ready to articulate some words, like *"Hey, don't you have something to say to me?"* I started to go into this meditative state to say, *"Oh God help him to see his wrong, and I will feel so much better."* Thankfully, I didn't say any of those things. That preacher never apologized for anything—and it was good for me because I needed to be humbled. When we are humbled, it reminds us not to repeat the mistakes that pride causes us to make the first time. If you want to handle your hands properly, you must deal with your pride. The only way to deal with pride is to kill it. If you leave it even a little bit alive, it will come roaring back to full health in no time.

The second cause of violence is a corrupt environment. We hear a lot of people worrying about the quality and cleanliness of our air and water these days. The government has agencies that test for pollutants and harmful chemicals. That's all well and good, but it is far more important to our spiritual health for us to worry about the cultural environment in which we find ourselves. Noah lived in a day which was much like our world today.

"And it came to pass, when men began to multiply on the face of the earth, and daughters were born unto them, That the sons of God saw the daughters of men that they were fair; and they took them wives of all which they chose. And the LORD said, My spirit shall not always strive with man, for that he also is flesh: yet his days shall be an hundred and twenty years. There were giants in the earth in those days; and also after that, when the sons of God came in unto the daughters of men, and they bare children to them, the same became mighty men which were of old, men of renown. And GOD saw that the wickedness of man was great in the earth, and that every imagination of the thoughts of his heart was only evil continually. And it repented the LORD that he had made man on the earth, and it grieved him at his heart. And the LORD said, I will destroy man whom I have created from the face of the earth; both man, and beast, and the creeping thing, and the fowls of the air; for it repenteth me that I have made them. But Noah found grace in the eyes of the LORD. These are the generations of Noah: Noah was a just man and perfect in his generations, and Noah walked with God. And Noah begat three sons, Shem, Ham, and Japheth. The earth also was corrupt before God, and the earth was filled with violence. And God looked upon the earth, and, behold, it was corrupt; for all flesh had corrupted his way upon the earth. And God said unto Noah, The end of all flesh is come before me; for the earth is filled with violence through them; and, behold, I will destroy them with the earth." (Genesis 6:1-13)

Whenever a society turns it back on God, violence is a natural result. There was a day in America when most people, whether they were saved or not, had a shared moral compass. The underlying truths of God's Word were part of our culture. They formed the basis for our system of laws and government. In those days, a woman could walk down the street at night without fear for her life. I remember when I was in high school and we would go to Detroit to watch the Tigers play baseball. We went places then that I'd be afraid to go as a grown man today. What has happened? As our society has become more and more corrupt, as we have turned our backs on God, removed the Bible and prayer form our schools, and overthrown His laws, we have also become more violent.

In Noah's day, he was the only preacher of righteousness. There wasn't anyone else encouraging people to do right. The sad truth is that today the number of preachers of righteousness is rapidly declining. There used to be men of God who stood behind the pulpits of our major cities and thundered against sin. When I was a little boy, Dr. G. B. Vick pastored the great Temple Baptist Church in downtown Detroit. It was an aggressive, soul-winning church. It is gone. You would be hard-pressed to find a Bible preaching voice in downtown Detroit today. No, our culture isn't what it used to be. But, the problem is not that Hollywood makes trashy television shows and worse movies. The problem is not that our politicians are corrupt and our country is in debt. The problem is not that the world doesn't know right from wrong. The problem is that God's people are not standing up and preaching righteousness. So, we should not be surprised that our society is becoming more and more violent.

The more corrupt an individual becomes, the more violent he

becomes. The more corrupt the family becomes, the more violent they become. The more corrupt the community becomes, the more violent it becomes. As the individual goes, so goes the family, so goes the community, and so goes the culture. I have great concern because holding a standard between right and wrong is fast disappearing, even in fundamental churches. We must never compromise on the truths of the book. The Bible is not a book about just how to feel good about yourself. Holiness is still in the Bible. There is still right, and there is still wrong. Our corrupt environment that leads to violence does not have to drag you down with it. Noah did right even when everyone else was doing wrong. Guard your family and your children. Hold the standards high. Be gentle with your hands, no matter what the rest of the world does.

The third cause of violence is a desire to get something for nothing. More than any other single thing, this is the leading cause of violence recorded in the pages of Scripture. Genesis 21:25 says, *"And Abraham reproved Abimelech because of a well of water, which Abimelech's servants had violently taken away."* In Abraham's day, wells were essential to maintaining large herds of cattle or sheep. They had to be dug by hand, thus wells were very labor intensive. Wells were guarded and protected because they were extremely valuable property. Could Abimelech's servants have done the hard work and dug their own well? Yes, but they didn't want to. Instead they wanted something for nothing. That attitude is infecting our nation today; and not only is it destroying our character, but it is leading to an increase in violence as well.

We have created a system in which people do not have to work.

I am not talking about people who are handicapped or disabled and cannot work; I'm talking about people who are not willing to work. Rather than allowing them to suffer the natural consequences of their sloth, we coddle and enable them. The problem is that not only do we give them a destructive philosophy of life, but we build a culture of violence as well. Once you have taught people to expect something for nothing, they are likely to respond with violence to get things they "deserve" but are not given. We are seeing riots around the world today in countries like Greece and England. People are burning police cars, looting stores, and beating and robbing people on the street. Why? The reason is because they aren't getting their handouts any more. This is not just a European phenomenon. It can and will happen here in America as well.

Knowing the danger of violence, we need to live humbly. When pride rears its ugly head, we need to cut it off immediately. Confess your sins rather than justifying your bad conduct. Guard your heart, your mind, your eyes, and your ears from the corrupt environment around us. Live righteously yourself and also encourage others to do so. We have the solution to their problems, and the only hope they have is to hear it from us. Finally, we must live contentedly within our means. A faith in God's presence in our lives helps us fight the urge to covet. (Hebrews 13:5) In order to be gentle, we must walk in the Spirit. Galatians 5:22 tells us that gentleness is a fruit of the Holy Spirit. As He works in your life, you can live in this world and handle your hands. With His help, we can be at peace among ourselves and be gentle men and gentle ladies.

CHAPTER SEVEN

APT TO TEACH

"And the servant of the Lord must not strive; but be gentle unto all men, apt to teach, patient, In meekness instructing those that oppose themselves; if God peradventure will give them repentance to the acknowledging of the truth; And that they may recover themselves out of the snare of the devil, who are taken captive by him at his will." (2 Timothy 2:24-26)

One of the great heroes of American education is Noah Webster. He is best known today for publishing the first American dictionary. Webster was a brilliant linguist. He established a system of rules to govern spelling, grammar, and punctuation for the American dialect of the English language. He understood the power of words, their definitions, and their need for precision in our word usage and our communication. In his famous 1828 dictionary, Noah Webster used the Bible as the foundation for his definitions. Why did he do that? It was because of his philosophy of education. Webster wrote, "In my view, the Christian religion is the most important and one of the first things in which all children under a free government ought to be instructed. No truth is more evident to my mind than that the Christian religion must be the basis of any government intended to secure the rights and privileges of a free people. Truly education is useless without the Bible." Clearly Noah Webster understood the value of a good teacher.

Our key verses on helping rescue those taken captive by the devilhighlight the importance of being "apt to teach." Notice that it is not just a teacher, but one who is apt to teach, that is needed. The value of a good and godly teacher cannot be overstated. You and I must become expert communicators of the truths which will instruct the prisoners of the spiritual war to escape from their captivity. This was first written of course to a preacher, Timothy, but it applies to every child of God who seeks to deliver captives. God wants to use our words, our instructions, and our teaching to help move and motivate them to say, "I want to go back to God. I want to do the right thing." Let me say this once more before we launch into the study of being apt to teach. Every believer is to be a teacher. Are you a parent? Are you a spouse? Are you a friend? Then there is someone you can and should be teaching, even if you never have a Sunday School class or pastor a church.

The things we have looked at so far, being gentle and not striving, are vital, as are the traits we will study later. But, none of those things matter if you are not willing and able to open your mouth and convey the truth effectively. We must grow in our aptitude to teach and to instruct others so that they might recover themselves out of the snare of the devil. So, let's examine some of the things Paul wrote to Timothy to prepare him for the ministry in order to learn how we can be apt to teach.

True understanding of teaching comes from God. In Second Timothy 2:7, Paul writes, *"Consider what I say; and the Lord give thee understanding in all things."* Do you think Paul was an effective teacher and communicator of truth? I do. He turned the world upside down. Despite all of his ability and skill, Paul did not rely on his own talents; but rather, he asked God to give Timothy understanding of what he had taught. We are only able to be effective in communicating the truth of the Word of God to others because of our co-instructor. This truth was so exciting to me when I discovered it as a young preacher. It is intimidating and overwhelming to consider taking an ancient book and opening its pages and talking to a diverse group of people—different ages, genders, spiritual gifts, personalities, social and economic levels, spiritual levels, saved and unsaved. Preaching one message that touches all of those people and their widely varying needs is an impossible human task. Thank God I don't have to do it by myself! When I pray before I preach, I often say something like, "May the Spirit of God apply this message to your heart today."

I remember as a young man that I was really struggling with the issue of music. The devil ensnared me with rock and roll. I knew that it was wrong, but I liked it. I enjoyed listening to it because of the emotional and physical effect it had on me. I remember sitting in church with my parents and thinking to myself, *"Doesn't this guy ever preach on anything besides rock music?"* Now, the truth is our pastor was against that ungodly junk, and he talked about it now and then, but most of the time he was preaching on something else entirely. It was the Spirit of God bringing conviction to my heart from the Word of God regarding my sin. Later on, I found out my sister Barbara was sitting under the same sermons, saying to herself, *"Doesn't this guy ever preach on anything besides reading romance novel?"* God, the Holy Spirit, took those messages and applied them to the different needs of our hearts. That is an exciting and motivational reality as we consider the communication of the truth of God's Word to others. Sometimes, we are reluctant because we say, "I can't answer other people's questions," or, "I don't know what their needs are." So what? God knows all the answers to the questions, and He knows what their needs are. The Holy Spirit of God can take your words and communicate the truth they need to hear at that particular moment to each individual.

Life-changing teaching comes from the Word of God. Second Timothy 2:9 says, *"Wherein I suffer trouble, as an evil doer, even unto bonds; but the word of God is not bound."* Paul wrote his second epistle to Timothy from his prison cell in Rome, not long before he was martyred for his faith. He was imprisoned like a common criminal. His movements were restricted. He could no longer travel across the Roman Empire and preach as he once had. Yet, even though Paul was in bondage, the power of the Word was not. The power of Paul's teaching was not found in his education, his rhetorical skills, or the force of his personality; it was found in the source of his message. Later on, Paul would tell Timothy, *"Preach the word; be instant in season, out of season; reprove, rebuke, exhort with all longsuffering and doctrine. For the time will come when they will not endure sound doctrine; but after their own lusts shall they heap to themselves teachers, having itching ears."* (2 Timothy 4:2&3)

We have certainly reached the day Paul foretold. Most people today do want to hear simple, straightforward, bold proclamation of the Word of God. They would rather have the preacher tell them all of the reasons to feel good about themselves and how to have their best life without any repentance or effort on their part. The only message that will help people who are in the snare of the devil is the pure and unadulterated preaching and teaching of the Word. Most Bible commentators believe that Timothy was probably in his early 20's when Paul sent him to pastor the church at Ephesus. How could such a young man hope to succeed in the ministry in a city filled with idol worship and immorality? Timothy was grounded in the Word of God. It filled his heart and mind, and had from a young age. Paul wrote, *"But continue thou in the things which thou hast learned and hast been assured of, knowing of whom thou hast learned them; And that from a child thou hast known the holy scriptures, which are able to make thee wise unto salvation through faith which is in Christ Jesus."* (2 Timothy 3:14&15) Timothy was no newcomer to the Scriptures. The fact that he could accurately and precisely and powerfully articulate the truths of God's Word is a testimony to the fact that he had been immersed in the Word of God. Timothy had a godly mother and a godly grandmother and she poured the Scripture into his heart and mind.

Effective teaching requires endurance. Paul wrote, *"Therefore I endure all things for the elect's sakes, that they may also obtain the salvation which is in Christ Jesus with eternal glory."* (2 Timothy 2:10) We sometimes act as if we have things pretty tough, but compared to what Paul endured, we have got it easy. He was shipwrecked, beaten, stoned, imprisoned, beaten some more, mocked, lied about, hunted, ridiculed, and left for dead. Why? It was because he continued to teach and preach the Word everywhere he went. No threatened or real danger could stop him. Paul was effective because he wouldn't quit. His concern for people—reaching those who were lost with the Gospel and rescuing those who were saved but ensnared—kept him going, even in the face of persecution and suffering. If you give up the first time you run into an obstacle or the person who does not respond as you think they should, you are not going to be an effective teacher.

By the way, it is very dangerous to remove yourself from the preaching and teaching of God's Word. A serious illness is one of the most dangerous times in a Christian's life. If you are not able to be in church regularly, you will be susceptible to falling into the snare of the devil. Why? There is something about the preaching and teaching of the Bible that is helpful in alerting us to danger and keeping us on track. Let me point out this truth--the best thing for people who are in the snare of the devil is exactly what they do not want to hear. They are not going to want to go to church. They are not going to want you to tell them the truth. Do it anyway!

Faithful teaching produces a reward. There is nothing more gratifying than seeing people come to Christ and be delivered out of the snares of the devil. I feel sorry for people who never get to see this happen. How discouraging that must be, because the Word of God is intended to be preached and taught in such a way that the Spirit of God can use it to change lives. And, the rewards are not just for this life alone. Second Timothy 2:12 says, *"If we suffer, we shall also reign with him."* There is a reward that comes to those servants of the Lord who are apt to teach, those who get involved and engaged in trying to get people to come to Christ and move on to spiritual maturity. You belong to the Lord, and you are His servant. As such, you should be busy doing what He wants you to do. God's business is the most important business in the world.

Hebrews 13:17 reminds those of us who have spiritual responsibility for others that one day we must give an account of our influence on them. I want to be an effective teacher so that I can give that account with joy. I am constantly aware that one day I will stand before the Lord, but I will not just stand there for Paul Kingsbury. I will stand there for the influence I have had on my wife, on my children, on my grandchildren, on our church, and all of those to whom I have ministered. More than anything else I want to hear the Father say, "Well done, good and faithful servant." If we want to receive the reward of faithful servants, then we must be willing to work and be consistent in our teaching and ministry. When we are teaching, there is Another present besides those we see with our eyes. We all are ministering before the Lord. That realization should motivate and stir us to be apt to teach.

Thank God for good and godly teachers, those who are apt to teach. I have some heroes in my life. My mom and dad are my heroes. I appreciate so much all of the investments they have made in my life. But, there are four men whose names are not household names by any means but who would also be right at the top of my list—Nicholas Weems, Mark Jackson, Arwan Reisch and Jim Alley. From conception till I was twenty-nine years of age, those four men were my pastors. They had a wonderful influence on my life through their teaching in ways I cannot begin to estimate. Those who are apt to teach have an opportunity for influence that is unparalleled in this world. May God help us to commit ourselves to this matter of being the best teachers that we can be of the truths of God's Word to help rescue those ensnared by Satan.

CHAPTER EIGHT

HOW TO BECOME A BETTER TEACHER

"And the servant of the Lord must not strive; but be gentle unto all men, apt to teach, patient, In meekness instructing those that oppose themselves; if God peradventure will give them repentance to the acknowledging of the truth; And that they may recover themselves out of the snare of the devil, who are taken captive by him at his will." (2 Timothy 2:24-26)

In the last chapter we saw how the vital role of being "apt to teach" is played in freeing captives from Satan's snares. I have seen the value of that gift over and over in my own life. I have been part of Bible teaching and preaching in fundamental churches since before I was born. As I have grown in grace and the knowledge of the Lord through the years, I have had the opportunity to see this gift in action. When I think back on my life, I am so grateful for those men and ladies who loved the Lord and loved me enough to be careful and able to communicate to me the truths of God's Word. There were times that I did not particularly want to hear what they had to say, but their teaching was useful and necessary in my spiritual growth and my development.

You have the opportunity to provide that same input and positive influence on the lives of others. In the verses that lead up to our key text for this study, Paul gives Timothy a series of instructions that are meant to equip him to be apt to teach. Great teachers come in all shapes and sizes. They have all kinds of voices. But, there is a common thread of great teaching that influences and impacts people. Beyond the direct power of God on the individual's life, the ability to speak logically, clearly, carefully, and compassionately has much to do with the care of the mind. As we look at this passage, we need to meditate on the highlighted commands, particularly as they relate to teaching.

*"**Study** to shew thyself approved unto God, a workman that needeth not to be ashamed, rightly dividing the word of truth. But **shun** profane and vain babblings: for they will increase unto more ungodliness. And their word will eat as doth a canker: of whom is Hymenaeus and Philetus; Nevertheless the foundation of God standeth sure, having this seal, The Lord knoweth them that are his. And, Let every one that nameth the name of Christ depart from iniquity. But in a great house there are not only vessels of gold and of silver, but also of wood and of earth; and some to honour, and some to dishonour. If a man therefore **purge** himself from these, he shall be a vessel unto honour, sanctified, and meet for the master's use, and prepared unto every good work. **Flee** also youthful lusts: but **follow** righteousness, faith, charity, peace, with them that call on the Lord out of a pure heart. But foolish and unlearned questions **avoid**, knowing that they do gender strifes."* (2 Timothy 2:15-23)

These are action commands for teachers; and if we follow them, they will guard our minds and improve our aptitude for teaching.

Philippians 2:5 tells us that we are to have the mind of Christ. How is that possible? The human mind is an amazing, God-designed computer, subject, just as all computers are, to the input it receives. If you and I are going to maximize our ability to be apt to teach, then we are going to have to properly care for our mind. The preparation of the mind begins with studying the right things. Though study is beneficial, the key to being an effective teacher is study of "the word of truth." The marvelous Scriptures are unlike any other book in all the libraries and in all the history of the world. The Bible is the Word of God. It does not simply contain the Word of God; it *is* the Word of God. From the very beginning to the end, from Genesis 1:1 to Revelation 22:21, the Bible is the Word of God. If you and I are going to hope to help people who are in the snare the devil, then we are going to have to study this marvelous book, the Bible. We must get to know the Word of God.

Have you recognized from the Scriptures that the Devil knows the Bible? He is willing to use it to tempt people—in fact, in the temptation of Christ, recorded in Luke chapter 4, Satan quoted from Psalm 91 to encourage Jesus to throw Himself off the pinnacle of the Temple. In the Garden of Eden, Satan began his conversation with Eve by questioning the words of God. *"Yea hath God said?"* he asked. Then, having created doubt in her mind, he denied the truth of what God said. *"Ye shall not surely die."* This was Satan's methodology in ancient times; this is Satan's methodology today. The only way that we can overcome his deception is by being students of the Word of God. This is not a one-time thing; it is a life-long process. Great teachers are and remain great students. They are willing to put the work into studying the Word. The word Paul uses here by inspiration carries the idea of being diligent. He is not talking about a casual study; he is talking about a thorough, sustained, intentional investment of time and resources in better learning the Word of God. If what you are doing does not take energy and thought and concerted effort, then you are probably not genuinely studying the Word of God.

Why are so many Christians today afraid to talk to cult members about the truth? Why are they unable to convince people of the truths of Scripture? Why are they confused by false doctrine and teaching? It is because they have not been good students, and they do not know the Word. We must recognize that our study and learning in the Word is not simply for our own benefit or so that people will think we are smart. We should study the Bible so that God looks at us and says, *"I approve of your work."* We should also study the Bible so that we will not be ashamed. How disheartening it is to not be able to help people who are ensnared because we do not know the truths of God's Word that could set them free. I am all for seeking godly counsel when you face a problem or difficulty, and I am not by any means saying you should not do that. However, you should not expect someone else to do all of your work for you. Shepherds don't feed healthy sheep—they take them to safe pastures where the grass is good. I sometimes tell people, "I can tell you what the Bible says, or I can tell you where to go in the Bible and how to study this out. Which would you like me to do?" There is a more significant impact on our minds when we research a subject in the Bible and discover it ourselves. Whatever your problem in life, you can find the answer in the Word of God.

Notice also that carefully approved study requires, *"rightly dividing the word of truth."* We are not to take the Bible and twist it to make it mean what we want it to mean. Rather, we are to carefully and accurately take the context, the meaning, and the truth God has for us from the Word. The idea of dividing here is the same concept you had in high school when you dissected a frog. You cut it open and look inside to see what is there. Study the books of the Bible all the way down to individual verses. Take the time and put forth the effort. The Bible describes us here as "workmen"—the word used for men who labored in the fields. Good study is hard work; but it is beneficial for our minds and enables us to not only live a better life personally, but also to be of use as teachers to others—especially those who are ensnared. When I started out in the ministry, I got a *Strong's Exhaustive Concordance of the Bible.* It was the biggest book in my whole library—and one I probably used the most. Another book I referred to often was *Vine's Expository Dictionary of New Testament Words* to get a better feel for the meaning of the words God chose to use in His Word. I also used the *Treasury of Scripture Knowledge,* with its extensive cross references to verses on the same topics. Today, there are marvelous computer programs like "Sword Searcher" that make it easier than ever before to be thorough in studying the Word.

A few years ago, I visited in the home of a brain surgeon. Over the course of our conversation, I found out that, though he was forty years old, he had only begun his practice a couple of years before. I asked, "You didn't begin your practice until you were in your late 30s. Did you get started late?" He replied, "Oh no, Pastor. Preparing to perform surgery on the human brain demanded years of schooling beyond even medical school." I thought about that. Here was a man who, because of the intricacies of the human brain and in order to properly perform surgery on that brain, was willing to pay the price going to college, going to medical school, and then going on for further training; because after all, he is dealing with the human brain. What excuse do we have for not being good students of the Word of God? The issues that we deal with are the eternal souls of men and women. To take shortcuts to hinder our ability to help others by our negligence in study of the Word of God is a shameful thing.

Let me say a special word to the pastors who are reading this. I think the reason in many places the sheep, I'm talking about the flock in the church, are anemic is because their ministers are so busy doing the nuts and bolts of the work of the Lord that they do not have time to give to concerted effort in studying the Word of God. I know there are few pastors who are just plain downright lazy and spend more time on the golf course than in the study, but that's not really who I want to address here. I want to sound the alarm to the diligent pastors who are getting wrapped up in the details of the work to the point where they are not studying the Word themselves. I have been in the ministry long enough to know that if I am going to stand up Sunday morning, Sunday night, and Wednesday night and have something fresh from the Lord to declare to my church, then I am going to have to work at it. It takes sacrifice, but it is worth it. Study and be diligent with the Scriptures.

Next, we see that to be better teachers, we are going to have to shun some things. We don't know much about Hymenaeus and Philetus, except that their teaching was enough of a problem to get them called out by name in Paul's epistle to Timothy. They apparently had gotten bogged down in empty and fruitless arguments and discussions. There were lots of words, but they didn't mean anything. That's a bad enough problem in itself, but Paul sounds a sober warning here. Allowing ourselves to be tangled up in empty and meaningless chatter "will increase unto more ungodliness." This is serious business. If our thinking is wrong, it will not be long before our conduct is wrong as well. Such conversation is a destructive and corrosive influence on our lives. One of the great benefits of being a part of a Bible believing and Bible preaching church and being a good student personally of the Word of God is that you will be alerted to false doctrine very, very rapidly. It is sad, but true, that there are many people who are saved, but they have been caught up in false teaching, in false doctrine, and false ways of thinking. As a result of not being good students of the Word of God and not staying in the Scriptures and under the sound teaching of the Word of God, they find themselves erring from the truth. Notice the progression: they first argue meaninglessly, then they find themselves living ungodly lives, and ultimately, they find their faith destroyed.

I have been preaching long enough to have met and ministered to thousands and thousands of people. We have been privileged in of our church to see many people come to Christ, and to see those who come grow and mature spiritually. One of the great sorrows of my life is that a number of people started out well but then got caught up in false doctrine and false teaching and have erred from the faith. It is a horrible thing; but if they had protected their minds, they could have shunned those vain babblings. You cannot just walk into a Christian bookstore and start picking out books. Just because the book says it is Christian does not mean it is Christ-centered. It does not mean that it is doctrinally correct. We need to be very, very careful even in the evangelical realm. There are books out there and authors out there who are very popular but whose philosophies have veered from the clear teaching of the Word of God. A couple of issues really disturb me on this front. The first is a trend toward casting doubt on the Word of God by coming up with a new Bible of the month. If you get saved and have the Holy Spirit of God living within you, you can take an 1828 Webster's Dictionary and the "archaic" King James Bible and understand what it says; and God can use it to speak to your heart. There is a great danger in coming out with these new translations. Unfortunately, many of the Bible colleges that once were solid have veered to the left in this very issue. I was talking to well-known evangelist not long ago. He had been forced to cancel meetings at certain Bible colleges because they have changed their position on the authority of the Word of God. It is the clear teaching of the Scriptures and our belief and understanding that God has not only given us His Word, but that He has preserved it for us in the English language in the Authorized Version of the Bible.

Secondly, many are getting caught up in a new wave of hyper-Calvinistic teaching. They are bringing in the teaching of John Piper from Minneapolis and others. These men are creating an atmosphere of "intellectualism" in the minds of the people who follow them. They look down on people like us who hold the traditional and historical position of fundamentalism. They mock people who simply believe that the Bible is the Word of God and interpret it in the simplest and most literal way possible. If you don't read and study the Bible that way, you will be led into all sorts of errors. Do not allow those teachings to enter your mind—shun them.

These issues are not just an end in themselves; they become a gateway that leads to all forms of ungodliness. I have watched good young men go off to seminaries and colleges and come back doubting the Word of God and having lost their zeal for God in their service for Him. This is the warning of the Scripture. If we are going to be good teachers of the Word of God, then we have to guard what comes into our minds.

Next, we see that there are some things which we must purge from our lives. If your house is like mine, then you have different kinds of dishes. You may have a set of china that you only eat from on special occasions. As well, you probably have a set of everyday dishes that you normally use. And most people probably have a stack of paper plates in the pantry somewhere that they use when making hamburgers or hotdogs and have a bunch of people over for a party. These are different vessels for different purposes, but they are all honorable. They serve the purpose for which they are intended. But, your house probably has some dishonorable vessels as well. We have a toilet bowl cleaner that we use for the purpose for which it was designed. But, suppose one night we were standing in the kitchen and my wife said, "I'm making stew and the spoon is dirty. Would you get me something else to use?" Then, I came back with the toilet bowl cleaner. Would you eat the stew? Why not?

If there are things in your life that are dishonorable, you need to purge them. Here is the problem—the dirt that is on the dishonorable vessel will contaminate everything else unless you remove it. If you have a silverware drawer full of clean forks and knives and spoons and then you take the toilet bowl cleaner and put it in the same drawer, what will happen? When you take it out, will the toilet bowl cleaner suddenly be clean and free of germs because it has been in the drawer with the spoons, the knives, and forks that were clean? No! Instead, the forks, the knives, and the spoons have been contaminated. The warning Paul sounds here is that there are people who will contaminate your faith, who will contaminate your mind, and who will contaminate the direction of your life. If you do not purge yourself of those ways of thinking, that literature, or those individuals, it will infect and affect you. Left unchecked, it will ultimately ruin your ability to be "apt to teach."

Then, Paul tells Timothy to **flee** and **follow**. There is a balance here, and neither one works without the other. Neither one alone will produce a powerful and effective teacher. Paul warned Timothy to flee from youthful lusts. When I first read that passage, I thought of the story of Joseph running to get away from Potiphar's wife. If you find yourself in that position, running away is a good thing, however that is not the primary meaning here. Lust takes place in our minds. It is an internal desire that we have. I've known some people who I thought might be out of their minds, but how do you flee from your own mind? The answer is that we must discipline ourselves to control our thoughts. Train yourself to run from impure thoughts to pure thoughts and from that which is wrong and evil, to that which is right and good.

If we are focused on righteousness, faith, charity, and peace, we will not find the things of the world to be as much of a temptation to us. Hebrews 11:15 says, *"And truly, if they had been mindful of that country from whence they came out, they might have had opportunity to have returned."* What this verse tells us is that if Abraham had been constantly looking over his shoulder, then he probably would have found a way to go back to the world he left behind. Instead, Abraham focused on following God as He led him to the "better country" He had promised. If you allow your mind to wander idly, it will inevitably wander to that which is evil. Instead, we need to live intentionally, following the good things of God and His grace. It will improve your life and your teaching as well.

Finally, Paul concludes by telling Timothy there are some things he should avoid. There is nothing gained by trying to answer a foolish question. If you are working to rescue those ensnared by Satan, you will probably run into some of those. People who do not want to leave the comfort of their snare will throw up all kinds of objections and "gotcha" questions to try to derail you. Avoid those questions. All they do is create strife. This is where the preparation of the mind of the teacher is so important. Your study and the leading of the Spirit of God will help you to skip the strife and stay focused on the issue at hand. What is on your mind, and how well are you caring for your mind today? The value of your mind and its purity, its clarity, its biblical basis, and its philosophy are essential to the success of your life and your ministry in helping to teach others so they may recover themselves out of the snare of the Devil.

CHAPTER NINE

THE ROOTS OF PATIENCE

"And the servant of the Lord must not strive; but be gentle unto all men, apt to teach, patient, In meekness instructing those that oppose themselves; if God peradventure will give them repentance to the acknowledging of the truth; And that they may recover themselves out of the snare of the devil, who are taken captive by him at his will." (2 Timothy 2:24-26)

The work of rescuing those ensnared by the Devil should be high on the priority list for every believer. Of course, not everyone cares enough to get involved and make the commitment to helping others, but we should. I like the philosophy of Charles Schultz, the creator of the "Peanuts" comic strip. In an article I read on his philosophy of life, he used a creative method to demonstrate how important it is that we genuinely care for people and get involved in their lives personally. When he would speak to a crowd, he began by asking six questions:

Can you name the five wealthiest people in the world?

Can you name the last five Heisman Trophy winners?

Can you name the last five ladies who were crowned Miss America?

Can you name five individuals who have won the Nobel Peace Prize?

Can you name five Academy award winners for best actor or best actress?

Can you name the last decade's worth of World Series winners?

Then, he would ask the crowd how they did in answering the questions. Their inability to recall all of the names reveals that the headlines that seem so important will one day quickly fade. Schultz did not ask about the runners up or the second place finishers, but he asked about the winners. Even the best in their fields find that the applause dies away, the awards tarnish, the achievements are forgotten, and the accolades and certificates mold and gather dust. Then, Schultz would come back with a second set of questions:

Name a teacher who aided you on your journey through education.

Name three friends who helped you through a difficult time in your life.

Name five people who have taught you something worthwhile.

Name five people that have made you feel appreciated and special.

Name five people that you enjoy spending time with.

People found those questions much easier to answer. Here is the lesson Charles Schultz said he wanted to get across: "The people that make the most difference in our lives are not the ones with the most credentials, the most money, or the most awards, but they are the ones that care." This is the core of our mission to rescue those who are ensnared—we must care for them. And, if we are to reach them, the next thing Paul tells us that we must be patient. Now, there may be someone somewhere for whom patience comes naturally, but I haven't met him yet. All of us need an extra dose or two of patience, and that need increases as we take on delivering captives from Satan.

There is a little phrase that I hate to hear when I'm on the phone. The person will say, "Just a minute." Whenever I hear those words, I know I'm in for a wait. It's even worse to hear it in person. I have noticed that if I am standing in line and the person says, "Just a minute," they always point up with their forefinger while they say it. I'm not sure what that adds to the situation, but it's pretty common. I hate to wait. Yet, Paul tells Timothy, and through him the Spirit of God also tells us, that we must be patient. To fully understand this instruction, we need to look at what the Bible means when it talks about patience. There are actually several different words for patience used in the Scriptures. By studying each of them, it will give us a better picture of God's idea of patience.

In Psalm 37:7, David, inspired by the Spirit of God, wrote, *"Rest in the Lord, and wait patiently for him."* The idea here is to not get in front of God. So many times we are tempted to take matters into our own hands and launch out on our own. However, the Hebrew root of this word for patience is very interesting. We find it in Judges 21, which is a strange story indeed, an illustration of how far people can and will go when they do what is right in their own eyes. This story actually reminds me a little of "Seven Brides for Seven Brothers." The men of Benjamin who do not have wives are told to go to a town named Shiloh, look for the unmarried women, pick one out, throw her over their shoulders and run for the hills. That's what they did. The Bible is not commending this method for finding a bride, it is simply recording that this is the way they did it. Judges 21:20&21 says, *"Therefore they commanded the children of Benjamin, saying, Go and lie in wait in the vineyards; And see, and, behold, if the daughters of Shiloh come out to dance in dances, then come ye out of the vineyards, and catch you every man his wife of the daughters of Shiloh, and go to the land of Benjamin."*

You might think that the Hebrew root word we are talking about in the context of patience is the one translated "lie in wait"; but instead, it is the word translated "dance." Before you go tell anyone that Pastor Kingsbury has lost his mind, and he is telling people to take up dancing, let me explain the underlying meaning. In the first place, this was not a ballroom waltz they were doing; they were basically leaping around in circles as part of a celebration. Still, how can the same word convey both "wait patiently" and "dance"? The idea of patience is to keep moving even if you're not making progress. To some people, patience is simply inactivity. Nothing could be further from the truth. God says, "No. If you understood what patience means, you would know that you need to keep dancing. I'm not calling you to inactivity, I'm compelling you to keep doing the things you know that you ought to keep doing and keep active and busy, even when it seems as if you are going around in circles and not making progress."

This is especially important when we consider it in the context of rescuing those who are ensnared. The temptation is to say, "They have gone to church and have heard the truth. They know the right thing to do. I'm just going to patiently wait for them to get right with God. I'm not going to do a thing." Rather, we should keep trying to help, keep reaching out, and keep speaking the truth in love. Yes, we are to be patient as we try to help, but that does not mean sitting back and coasting. Just keep doing what you are supposed to be doing. Keep dancing—staying in your place and moving—even through the hurts and frustrations and setbacks and circumstances. Do not judge by appearances whether anything is happening. Trust God to produce the harvest.

The second Hebrew word for patience is found in David's wonderful Psalm of testimony. Psalm 40:1 says, *"I waited patiently for the LORD."* This is not the same word used in Psalm 37. We can better understand the meaning of this word by looking at another place where it is used in Scripture, in the story of the Creation. In Genesis 1:9, we read, *"And God said, Let the waters under the heaven be gathered together unto one place, and let the dry land appear: and it was so."* The Hebrew word for patience here is translated in our English Bible as "gathered together in one." The idea here is to "hold it together." Impatience messes with our minds. I have seen this process work in my own life. When we are frustrated because someone is not cooperating not doing the right thing, we are in danger of becoming so frustrated that we come apart ourselves. I've seen it happen. We lose it mentally. We lose it emotionally. We lose it financially. Our physical health and spiritual balance and even taking care of our business and personal life can all suffer.

I have seen it happen more than once. A good Christian has been living with a family member who has a serious problem. They are doing their best to rescue their loved one from the snare of the enemy; but as time passes, rather than remaining patient, they crumble. They stop coming to church themselves, they stop reading the Bible and praying, and everything falls apart. Lifeguards are warned of one particular danger they face when they try to rescue a drowning person—the danger of being pulled under themselves. The devil is a raging and roaring lion, and we will be more than happy to get you while you are trying to rescue someone else. Be on your guard, be patient, and hold it together.

There is a third Hebrew word for patient used by Solomon. Ecclesiastes 7:8 says, *"Better is the end of a thing than the beginning thereof: and the patient in spirit is better than the proud in spirit."* As with our first two examples, this word also has another connotation that allows us to see more fully what God expects from us. Ezekiel 17:3 says, *"And say, Thus saith the Lord GOD; A great eagle with great wings, longwinged, full of feathers, which had divers colours, came unto Lebanon, and took the highest branch of the cedar."* You would never pick this one out just by looking at the English, but the Hebrew word is the one translated for us as "longwinged." At first glance that does not seem to have anything to do with patience, but take a moment and consider the eagle with me. Eagles have wingspans that can reach up to nine feet. It is those huge wings that allow the eagle to soar effortlessly for great lengths of time. The length of their wings allows them to catch even the smallest updrafts of the wind.

That is a beautiful picture of how patience works. If we have it, we catch even the smallest indications of hope and progress and use them to keep us going in the right direction. An eagle's wings don't get discouraged because there isn't a lot of air moving—even a little keeps them going. It is also interesting to me that the eagle does not frantically flap its wings. Each beat of those long and powerful wings takes the eagle a long way through the air. When you are working with someone who is ensnared, keep on soaring. Do not let anything drag you down. Be patient, and trust God to bring the results.

There are also two Greek words used in the New Testament for patience that we need to understand. The first is used in the parable Jesus told of a servant who owed a great deal of money and had no way to pay it back. Matthew 18:26 says, *"The servant therefore fell down, and worshipped him, saying, Lord, have patience with me, and I will pay thee all."* Of course, as you know in the story, though this man asked for patience for himself, he did not extend it to others. The Greek word is a compound word, made up from the words "long" and "breathing hard." The idea behind it is that there should be a long distance or a long period of time before we get to the place where we cannot control our physical reaction, because we are so angry about what is going on. Patience allows time for things to work themselves out, while still remaining in control of feelings and actions.

The second word was used by Jesus when He explained to the disciples the meaning of the parable of the sower. Jesus described each of the four types of soil onto which the seed fell, ending with the good soil that produced a harvest. *"But that on the good ground are they, which in an honest and good heart, having heard the word, keep it, and bring forth fruit with patience.* (Luke 8:15) If we are going to become fruitful Christians, it will take more than just getting saved. You do not plant a seed today and go and reap a harvest tomorrow.

It takes time for the results and the harvest to come. Like the word used in Matthew 18, this also is a compound word. The first means "cheerful, filled with hope" and the second means "to endure without ever quitting." We see here that patience is more than just our actions. It encompasses our attitude as well.

Have you ever had someone who had a bad attitude try to help you? It does not take long for you to decide that it isn't worth having the help to put up with the way they are acting. That can also happen with the people we are trying to help—our attitude can overcome our intention, and our lack of cheerful waiting can keep us from being able to rescue them. God tells us to be patient—keep dancing, hold it all together, stay aloft, don't lose your cool, and enjoy life cheerfully without giving up. That is what God's idea of patience looks like. Some of us are clock people. We want to see results right now. We want people to break the bonds and escape the snares in time for us to be home for dinner. But, it does not always work that way. Instead, we need to be calendar people. Rescuing those ensnared by Satan takes time. Be patient. If you are patient, then you have a great possibility of being able to influence somebody that you are trying to help.

As we close this study of patience, we must see the perfect example—God Himself. God brought the children of Israel out of the land of Egypt miraculously and delivered them from bondage. When they reached Mount Sinai, He called Moses up on the mountain to give him the Ten Commandments. While Moses was gone, Aaron made a golden calf and the people have a party. They took off their clothes and started playing bad music. They had an orgy. (They had come out of Egypt, but Egypt had not come out of them.) It is unbelievable that people God had delivered would act that way—but how many times do we do the same thing? God was angry, and He told Moses that He was going to destroy the people and start over. Moses fell on his face and beseeched God for mercy. He pleaded with the Lord and said, "Please don't do that." God did not destroy His people—because it is His nature to be patient. This is how He described Himself to Moses. *"And the LORD passed by before him, and proclaimed, The LORD, The LORD God, merciful and gracious, longsuffering, and abundant in goodness and truth, Keeping mercy for thousands, forgiving iniquity and transgression and sin."* (Exodus 34:6) Without God's patience, you and I would have been rightly destroyed long ago. Having received that patience, we should show the same mercy to others. This is what it takes to influence people to repent and recover themselves out of the snare of the Devil.

CHAPTER TEN

HOW TO GAIN WAIT

"And the servant of the Lord must not strive; but be gentle unto all men, apt to teach, patient, In meekness instructing those that oppose themselves; if God peradventure will give them repentance to the acknowledging of the truth; And that they may recover themselves out of the snare of the devil, who are taken captive by him at his will." (2 Timothy 2:24-26)

Someone said that the only place impatiens is beautiful is in the garden. I think whoever said that was right! The truth is that impatience is not a learned behavior. We never say to a child who is screaming because he didn't get what he wanted, "Where did you learn such good impatience?" It comes naturally to each one of us. Impatience is part of the fallen sin nature we inherited from Adam, and it is refined as we continue to exercise and use it throughout our lives. Patience is the trait that must be learned. Patience must be acquired. It must be developed. It is not in our nature that we be patient. Yet, patience is a vital component of our Christian life and ministry, particularly to those who are ensnared by the devil. Patience does not come with age, it does not come with practice, it does not come with need—it comes when we learn it. So, let's look at the Bible plan to learn patience, or to "gain wait."

Let me say this right up front. Patience is not an academic subject. We do not learn it in a classroom or at a seminar. If you want to learn a language, you learn the parts of speech, the rules of grammar, and the spelling and punctuation. You learn a language by study. In contrast, if you want to learn to play the piano, you practice. Yes, you need to learn the different notes and the rules of music and the scale. However, the bulk of your time is spent with your hands on the keyboard. Patience is like that. It requires practice—lots and lots and lots of practice. Patience is a hard thing to learn, but it is so valuable, both in our own life and in terms of ministering to others. As we saw in the last chapter, patience is the key to bringing forth fruit in our lives. (Luke 8:15) No one ever grows spiritually themselves or ministers effectively to others unless they first learn patience. So, let's look at how the Bible says we should go about acquiring this difficult, but necessary, character trait.

First, **patience requires that we maintain control over ourselves**. Luke 21:19 says, *"In your patience possess ye your souls."* When the Bible refers to the soul, it means you as a being. It is usually a reference to our mind, our will, and our emotions; though it can also mean our physical life, or the whole of us as a human being. So, when Jesus said to "possess" our souls, He was saying, "In patience remain in control of your emotions. In patience remain in control over your will. In patience remain in control of your physical life." Many people suffer devastating consequences that can be directly traced to a lack of patience. If you find yourself getting angry and frustrated as you work with others, then you need to work on your patience. It is a vital tool to achieving God's purpose in your life.

Second, **we need patience to receive God's promises**. The Bible is filled with many wonderful promises, but we know that not everyone takes full advantage of them. Hebrews 6:11&12 says, *"And we desire that every one of you do shew the same diligence to the full assurance of hope unto the end: That ye be not slothful, but followers of them who through faith and patience inherit the promises."* The promises of God are certain and sure, but they are not always immediate. Just as a farmer must wait after he plants a seed to reap the harvest, receiving God's promises requires a measure of faith and patience. This truth is illustrated in the life of Abraham. God called him to leave his home and go to a new country and promised him that he would have a sign. Was the promise true? Of course. But it took a very long time before it happened. Abraham is called the father of the faithful because he had enough patience to continue believing until he received the fulfillment of the promises. Hebrews 6:15 says, *"And so, after he had patiently endured, he obtained the promise."*

Of course, Abraham did not always have patience. Many years passed between the time that God promised him a son and the birth of Isaac. We can short-circuit the process and never realize the promise of God because we are not patient in waiting. As the years passed by and their biological clocks kept ticking, Sarah told her husband, "I have this servant girl who takes care of me. I'm going to go ahead and let you have relations with her, and maybe I can have a baby through her." Abraham said, "That sounds good to me." That is not what God had told him to do though. Because of his impatience with God, Abraham went ahead and had relations with Hagar, and what happened? She did get pregnant. She had a son, and they named him Ishmael. Ishmael eventually became the leader of a great tribe. He had twelve sons of his own. That tribe expanded and grew to become the Arab peoples of today. Think about it, one man and one woman's disobedience, their disregard, their absence of patience, had repercussions that still continue thousands of years later. Yet, in Hebrews 11, God leaves out that part of the story. It is not that God forgot; it is that blood of Jesus Christ covers all of our sins.

Third, **we cannot finish well without patience**. Someone said, "The Christian life is not a sprint, it is a marathon," and I believe that is true. First Peter 2:20b says, *"…when ye do well, and suffer for it, ye take it patiently, this is acceptable with God."* You will find as you study the Bible that patient people remarkably mature. Paul had problems with some of the people in the church at Corinth. Because they did not want to hear his correction, they challenged his credentials as an apostle. When Paul wanted to give them a list of his qualifications as a minister of the Gospel, guess what the first thing on the list was? Second Corinthians 6:4&5 says, *"But in all things approving ourselves as the ministers of God, in much patience, in afflictions, in necessities, in distresses, In stripes, in imprisonments, in tumults, in labours, in watchings, in fastings."* Later, he says, in Second Corinthians 12:12, *"Truly the signs of an apostle were wrought among you in all patience, in signs, and wonders, and mighty deeds."*

Fourth, **we see that suffering is key to developing patience**. When James in his epistle brought up the subject of patience, he used the life of Job as an illustration. If you read the Bible, you will find very few individuals who possessed extraordinary patience. I think that is a reminder of just how challenging it is to become a habitually patient person. James wrote, *"Behold, the husbandman waiteth for the precious fruit of the earth, and hath long patience for it, until he receive the early and latter rain. Be ye also patient; stablish your hearts: for the coming of the Lord draweth nigh. Grudge not one against another, brethren, lest ye be condemned: behold, the judge standeth before the door. Take, my brethren, the prophets, who have spoken in the name of the Lord, for an example of suffering affliction, and of patience. Behold, we count them happy which endure. Ye have heard of the patience of Job, and have seen the end of the Lord; that the Lord is very pitiful, and of tender mercy."* (James 5:7-11)

Think about the implications of what the passage tells us concerning this matter of becoming an example of patience. How did Job become a remarkably, honorably, patient man? Job had to suffer affliction. Wherever you see in the Bible a statement concerning someone's patience, you will inevitably find somewhere a reference made to some awful pain, some intense suffering, oftentimes inexplicable in the individual's life. There was no earthly explanation for the suffering Job experienced. In one fell swoop, on one single day, Job lost everything. One after another, his servants came running in to give him the bad news that another part of his assets had been lost. His oxen were stolen, then his sheep were killed, and then his camels were stolen. Finally, he received the devastating news that all of his children were dead as well. Even that was not enough for Satan. He returned to God and asked for permission to do even more to Job, and God granted his request. Now, Job was afflicted with boils from the very top of his head to the bottom of his feet. The only relief that Job could find was to sit by the fire and open up those sores and let the puss out and he would take the embers and coals from the fire and cauterize the wound to minimize the pain. It is almost humanly incomprehensible. On top of that, Job's wife and friends turned out to not be much help either. The next time you are tempted to complain about how tough you have it, compare your situation to Job.

Every person, every problem, and every pain, all the afflictions that God allows into our lives, may have other purposes. But, one purpose is sure in affliction, you and I may become more patient. I have heard people say, "Well, I never pray for patience, because you know what happens when you pray for patience—trouble comes." I have studied this subject thoroughly, and I have some news for you. Whether you pray for patience or not, trouble is going to come. There is no way to avoid it. God allows various afflictions into our lives to develop us, particularly in the area of patience. Job had no idea through all that happened that he was on display. He had no idea that God and Satan had a conversation about him. As far as we know from what is recorded in the book of Job, he never found out until he reached Heaven. I have no idea who is watching your life and mine, but someone is watching. The way that we respond to adversity and the way we respond to various afflictions of life, particularly our response to those afflictions which have no apparent cause. They are not a chastisement for doing wrong, but they are an opportunity for us to display God's grace in our lives.

Finally **we see that patience is a choice.** James 1:4 says, *"But let* *patience have her perfect work, that ye may be perfect and entire, wanting nothing."* Just as Job did, we have a choice when we go through affliction. Affliction is not a choice, we will go through that. But we can either allow patience to work, or we can bail out on the process and miss out on the lessons God is trying to teach us to benefit our own lives and to help others as well. Job made another choice as well. Though his friends had falsely accused him of all sorts of evil things, Job not only forgave them, but he also prayed for them. It was at that point that God began to restore all that Job had lost. Are you holding a grudge over how someone treated you today? You will remain in bondage until you choose to let it go. When you come to the end of the story of Job, you see that patience was developed in this man's life. Job was rewarded by God giving him double all that he had lost. We all should desire more patience in our lives.

I heard a story about a man who was in the grocery store, walking down the cookie aisle. He saw a woman with a three-year-old girl in she shopping cart. As he passed them, the little girl began to fuss and whine as she went by the cookies. The mother said quietly, "Ellen we just have half the aisles to go through. Don't get upset. It won't be long." He passed the same mother again in the candy aisle of the grocery store. The girl, seeing the candy, started to shout; and when she was told that she couldn't have any candy, she began to cry. Again, he overheard the mother say, "Ellen, don't cry. Only two more aisles to go, then we will be checking out." He happened to be behind her at the checkout counter and the little girl began to clamor for gum. When she was not allowed to have any gum, she burst into tears and threw a terrible tantrum. The mother patiently said, "Ellen, we will be through this checkout stand in a couple of minutes, and then you can go home and have a nice nap." The man followed them out to the parking lot, and he stopped the woman. He was so anxious to complement her. He said, "Ma'am, I couldn't help but noticing how patient you were with little Ellen." The mother replied, "Little Ellen? I'm Ellen; my little girl's name is Tammy!"

Sometimes, you may just have to talk to yourself and remind yourself to keep going. There may be just two more aisles, just five more minutes, and then you can take a nap. It will not be long before this is all over. When we are on the other side, we will be ashamed of those times when we made terrible decisions because of our impatience; and we will rejoice in those trials that God brought into our lives to develop and mature us to be more patient, so that we could enjoy and appreciate His blessings. Be patient, do not step ahead of God, and do not put yourself in a bind. Sometimes, in our lives we say, "I'd love to have these blessings of the Lord in my life economically," or "I would like to have the blessings of the Lord on my family." You are going to have to be patient to see those blessings. You are going to have to endure afflictions. Things are going to happen. They happened in Job's family, and they will happen in your family. Rather than becoming bitter, allow God to mature you through those afflictions and accept them from His hand. God will be a debtor to no man, and He will reward us richly for our patience.

CHAPTER ELEVEN

MEEKNESS IS NOT WEAKNESS

"And the servant of the Lord must not strive; but be gentle unto all men, apt to teach, patient, In meekness instructing those that oppose themselves; if God peradventure will give them repentance to the acknowledging of the truth; And that they may recover themselves out of the snare of the devil, who are taken captive by him at his will." (2 Timothy 2:24-26)

We have both a corporate responsibility as a local church and individual responsibility as believers to be servants of the Lord. We are not here to serve ourselves, and we are not here merely to serve one another; we are here to serve the Lord. And, as servants of the Lord, we have the obligation to rescue those ensnared by the devil. We have been looking at the traits that make us effective in this vital task, and now we come to the subject of meekness. This is another godly trait that is so misunderstood by our culture. Meekness is not weakness. Meekness is the yielding of one's rights for the benefit of others and for the glory of God. Weakness is a yielding of one's responsibilities to make things better and easier for self. There is a vast difference between the two. In the war for recovery, we must practice Biblical meekness.

To help you understand the Bible concept of meekness, I want you to think back to your Driver's Education class. If your class was anything like mine, one of the things they focused on teaching us was defensive driving. When you drive defensively, you yield the right-of-way. It may be your turn to go at the intersection, but you do not insist on your rights. That is meekness. Your light may be green, but if there is a big Mack truck barreling down the road showing no signs of stopping, I would advise you to yield! Do you have the right to pull out? Of course. Is it the wise thing to do? No. If you insist on your rights, you may find out what the inside of an ambulance looks like up close. Even worse, your family may find out what the inside of the funeral home looks like. You are not being weak or foolish by yielding, you are being meek.

A relationship without meekness is bound for trouble. I saw a cartoon that so brilliantly depicted this problem. There were two mules tied together by a rope. There was a bale of hay in front of each mule, and each of them was pulling with all his might to reach "his" bale of hay. If they had stopped working against each other and simply worked together, they could have had plenty of hay. The caption of the cartoon said, "When no one yields, no one wins." Meekness matters. If you are going to help people who are ensnared to find their way to freedom, then you must teach them in a spirit of meekness. There are many traits that go into being a good teacher. It helps to know your subject well. It helps to be articulate and able to convey truth in a way that is understandable. It is important to be able to motivate your students, so that they want to learn and put into practice what you teach them. All of those traits are good and important; but when God picked an adjective for an effective instructor, He chose meekness. Effective teaching springs from a meek spirit.

The church at Corinth had numerous problems. If you read Paul's letters to them, especially the first one, they are filled with correction. Paul, writing by the inspiration of the Holy Spirit of God, pulled no punches. He named the sins they were tolerating and pointed out those who needed to be disciplined by the church. Yet, in First Corinthians 4:21, Paul says, *"What will ye? shall I come unto you with a rod, or in love, and in the spirit of meekness?"* Even correction can and should be done meekly. Galatians 6:1 says, *"Brethren, if a man be overtaken in a fault, ye which are spiritual, restore such an one in the spirit of meekness; considering thyself, lest thou also be tempted."* A meek spirit on our part allows those we are trying to help to listen to the message rather than feeling they are being attacked and must defend themselves. Remember that meekness is a fruit of the Spirit according to Galatians 5:23. It comes as we walk after the Spirit in obedience to God's will as revealed in His Word and yield our rights for God's glory and the good of others.

When the Holy Spirit chose an example of meekness to set before us in the Word, He used the life of Moses as an illustration. Numbers 12:3 says, *"(Now the man Moses was very meek, above all the men which were upon the face of the earth.)"* Moses was a man of great strength, of great purpose, of great courage, of great determination. He was not afraid to tackle the hard subjects or the hard projects. He took them all on, but he was also a man of whom it could be said that he was the meekest man on the face of the earth. Meekness is demonstrated best in adverse conditions. Moses made great sacrifices and took great risks to lead the people out of bondage in Egypt. Despite that, they did not appreciate him. You will not find a record of a special "Moses Day" where they honored Moses. Instead, they were always griping and always complaining. They were vicious in their attacks on Moses. Yet, as you read through Scripture, you do not find Moses defending himself. This was true even when his own brother and sister turned on him.

Miriam and Aaron did not approve of Moses' wife because she was an Ethiopian, and they publicly criticized him for marrying her. Listen to their complaint against Moses. "Who does he think he is? Does he think that God only speaks through him?" They began to attack their own brother, which is ironic because they would not have even had the privilege of leadership that they had if it had not been for Moses. Moses could have stood up and said, "Listen, Miriam and Aaron. Shut your mouths!" He could have said, "Go back to Egypt." Instead, Moses was quiet, so God said, "I am going to speak up." The beauty of meekness is that God comes to the defense of the meek. I would rather have God on my defense team than any other lawyer. God called Miriam, Aaron, and Moses to come outside the camp. God rebuked Miriam and Aaron. Apparently, Miriam was the instigator of the complaint, and God struck her with leprosy. Moses cried out to God to forgive her; and after seven days, his sister was healed.

Meekness is a spirit. It is an attitude of yielding. The Greek scholar William Vine, said concerning meekness, "It is a spirit by which we accept God's dealings with us as good, without disputing or resistance." The spirit of meekness sees even insults and oppositions by evil men as permitted by and employed by God for His purposes. This view allows a person with a spirit of meekness to not insist on having his own way or insist on having his rights. These individuals have reached a place in their lives where they have such an amazing trust in God and in His providence and in His sovereignty that they can say, "I understand that whatever happens to me, God is in control. God has purposes that I cannot see. So why should I resist?" I am not talking about abdicating responsibility—that is weakness, not meekness. God knows we have plenty of weak Christians; Christians who say, "I don't want to get involved, I'm not going to get engaged," in areas where God has called all of us to be involved. That is weakness.

The Bible says that when Jesus taught, He taught as one having authority. (Matthew 7:29) While meekness is not weak, it also is not harsh. Some preachers and people in their dealings with others try to motivate them to do the right thing; but instead, they often become carnal, vicious, crass, rude, and even crude. I have seen it and heard it. I have to admit there have been times early in my ministry when I used harshness as a tactic, trying to insult people into doing the right thing. That never works. While Jesus taught with authority and confidence, He never exhibited the pompous, arrogant, insulting nature which seems to well up when we feel that those we are trying to help are not "getting it" fast enough. This kind of thinking is rooted in selfishness; a mindset that thinks God and others owe us something. Left unchecked, this spirit will destroy your effectiveness in ministering to others. True freedom is ultimately found in Jesus Christ. When we are rightly related to Him, we need not insist upon our rights. I am not talking about responsibilities, obligations, and duties; I am talking about the yielding of what we perceive to be our rights.

This same pattern applies to all of our relationships. Peter, writing to a group of people where many wives had converted to Christianity, but their husbands had not, spoke of the importance of meekness. *"Likewise, ye wives, be in subjection to your own husbands; that, if any obey not the word, they also may without the word be won by the conversation of the wives; While they behold your chaste conversation coupled with fear. Whose adorning let it not be that outward adorning of plaiting the hair, and of wearing of gold, or of putting on of apparel; But let it be the hidden man of the heart, in that which is not corruptible, even the ornament of a meek and quiet spirit, which is in the sight of God of great price."* (1 Peter 3:1-4) If you insist upon your rights, then you are not going to get anywhere in reaching others. If in meekness you yield, not to wrong, but what we perceive to be our rights, then we maximize the possibility of the person we are trying to help to listen to the voice of God and the voice of reason.

There is a wonderful example in the Old Testament of this kind of spirit in action. In Genesis 13, we find that both Abraham and Lot's herds were growing; and as a result, there was the strife between their herdsmen. Abraham called his nephew and said, "Lot, let's talk. Let's not have strife between our herdsmen. We have so many cattle and sheep that there is not enough room for all of us here." Abraham had the right to say, "Lot, I'm going to take this land, and you can have that land." He had that right, legally, ethically, and morally, but what did he do? He told Lot that he was yielding his right of first choice to him. I can imagine some of Abraham's servants said, "That weak Abraham, that dullard. That guy is a spineless wimp. He should have insisted on the best land." Abraham did not insist on his rights because wanted to maximize his ability to be spiritually close to his nephew. Lot took advantage of Abraham yielding (and that will sometimes happen if you are working with someone who is ensnared by Satan) and chose the well watered plains—the best land for cattle and sheep. He said, "If you're going to give it to me, then I'm going to take it." Lot walked away smiling. If the story stopped there, we would think that Abraham was foolish, and Lot was wise. But, the story does not stop there.

Lot's insistence on his rights led to disaster for his entire family. He drifted into Sodom and became wrapped up in the affairs of that evil city. His daughters married heathen men, and when he did finally warn them that judgment was coming, they laughed at him. His wife turned into a pillar of salt because she looked back to the evil city where her heart was. Lot lay in drunken incest with two of his daughters, and sired the fathers of the Moabites and Ammonites—enemies of the nation of Israel for generations. Do you really want to insist on your rights? Do you really want to make a point of getting what you deserve? Would it not be better to say instead, "I'm going to defer to you"?

Not only did Lot's choice lead to disaster, but Abraham's choice led to blessing, for himself and for his family in the future. Abraham taught the importance of meekness to his son Isaac as well. In Genesis 26, we find the story of a conflict between Isaac and the Philistines. Isaac had his servants dig a well to provide water for the animals and the people. The Philistines came and filled the well in with dirt by night. Isaac woke up and saw what they had done, so he moved his whole family and dug another well. The Philistines found out about it, snuck in, and filled that well too. Isaac got up and moved again and dug a third well. You say, "He should have insisted on his rights." It was a lot of work to dig a well by hand. He could have stood his ground. But, that would have been a disastrous decision. Isaac and his men were no match for the Philistines. They would have been wiped off the face of the earth. Eventually, the Philistines figured it out. They said, "This guy is persistent. He is not going to react and give us a cause to wipe them out. He is just going to keep digging these wells. We might as well leave him alone." Isaac said, "That's all I wanted." By his deference and meekness, Isaac received peace with the Philistines.

Do you have someone with whom you need to be at peace? Do you have someone who needs your instruction, your help, your tutelage, your influence? Seek to yield where you can, with the spirit of trusting God to take care of you. You may find this approach will melt the hardened hearts and bring that individual to a place of yielding themselves. I think one of the greatest presidents in the history of our country was President Abraham Lincoln. Carl Sandburg, the poet, wrote of Abraham Lincoln that, "Not often in the story of mankind does a man arrive on Earth who is both steel and velvet, who is as hard as rock and as soft as drifting fog, who holds in his heart and mind the paradox of a terrible storm and peace, unspeakable and perfect." Abraham Lincoln demonstrated on every hand during the tumultuous years of the Civil War both the qualities of a man of steel, and yet also a man with a velvet heart. When the Civil War ended, the great General Robert E. Lee surrendered his army to General Ulysses S. Grant. Abraham Lincoln sent a message to the enemy commander. "Tell your men they may keep their horses. They will need them for plowing. And tell your men they may keep their rifles. They will need them for hunting." That is the spirit of meekness. May God give us that spirit as we work with those who have been captured by Satan that they may recover themselves from his snares.

CHAPTER TWELVE

MEEKNESS: THE BYPRODUCT OF ADVERSITY

"And the servant of the Lord must not strive; but be gentle unto all men, apt to teach, patient, In meekness instructing those that oppose themselves; if God peradventure will give them repentance to the acknowledging of the truth; And that they may recover themselves out of the snare of the devil, who are taken captive by him at his will." (2 Timothy 2:24-26)

Having looked at the importance of meekness in our teaching about the ministry of recovery, now let's look at the way in which meekness can be developed and built in our lives. Again, it is impossible to overstate the importance of meekness to this vital work. It is a pity to know your subject well, be able to articulate it in an interesting, creative, and helpful way; and yet not be able to accomplish your goal because of your own personal lack of meekness. I'm reminded of what American essayist Ralph Waldo Emerson wrote a about a young and inexperienced ministerial student who came to his church. "Long on homiletic training and short on experience." Emerson complained that his sermons, though they were doctrinally correct, were delivered by a means that was cold and calculated. In fact, he said, "The poor man had not one word intimating that he had ever laughed or wept. We could not have known he was married or had ever even been in love, had ever been commended, cheated, or chagrined. If he had ever lived or acted we were none the wiser for it. The capital secret of his profession, to convert life into truth, he had not yet learned. Not one fact in all of his experience had he imported into his doctrine. There was not a surmise or a hint in all of the discourse that he had lived at all. We heard the truths but not through the life message of the individual. A line was not drawn out from personal history. I am of the personal opinion that the true preacher can be known by this, that he deals out the Word of God to people through life experience that he himself has gone through."

It is not enough to be right. It is important to be proper and doctrinally sound; but if our approach lacks personal empathy, if it lacks an understanding and a grasp of the seriousness and the sorrow and the pain that the individual is going through, then it will lack the power to soften the hardened heart. Our Savior came to earth not only to die for our sins; but He came, so that through His redemption, we would become sons and daughters of God by grace through faith. He also came so that He might be a sympathetic high priest who could identify with us in our temptations, our trials, and our sorrows. It behooved Him, the Bible says in Hebrews 2:17, to be made like unto His brethren. That means it was necessary for Jesus to become a man. Why? It was necessary so that He could, when we cry out to Him, turn to the Father, and say, "Father, I understand."

Empathy and sympathy comes through a spirit of meekness. Jesus chose to describe Himself that way. He said, "I am meek and lowly in heart." (Matthew 11:29)

If meekness was so important to the life and ministry of Jesus, then it should be no surprise to find that it is so important to those who will be instructors of God's truth to help recover those who are ensnared by Satan. Albert Barnes, the great Bible expositor said, "With a kind and forbearing and forgiving spirit, we must help those that have been overtaken, not with anger, not with a lordly and overbearing mind, not with the love of finding fault with others, not with a harsh temper but with love and gentleness and humility and patience and with the readiness to forgive when wrong has been done. No man should ever attempt to admonish or rebuke another who cannot do it in a spirit of meekness." That raises the question: How is a spirit of meekness achieved? Paul uses the analogy of putting on clothes in his letter to the church at Colosse. Colossians 3:12&13 says, *"Put on therefore, as the elect of God, holy and beloved, bowels of mercies, kindness, humbleness of mind, meekness, longsuffering; Forbearing one another, and forgiving one another, if any man have a quarrel against any: even as Christ forgave you, so also do ye. And above all these things put on charity, which is the bond of perfectness."* When you get dressed in the morning, you decide what clothes to wear. What shirt matches this suit, and what tie should I wear with it? How do we clothe ourselves in meekness? We choose to put it on.

It is important to remember that while we have a personal responsibility to choose meekness, we are not expected to come up with it on our own. That is a good thing, because if we were expected to manufacture meekness ourselves, we would fail miserably. When I got saved on the third Sunday night of March 1959, I did not know I had a new person living inside me. I did not realize then that God came to dwell in my heart. The person of the Holy Spirit took up residence in my life; and, of course, He has every quality of the Godhead, of the Father and Son, and all the power to enable me to live for Christ. And, one of the things He produces in my life is meekness. (Galatians 5:23) Meekness is His fruit, but I must allow it to be produced. Galatians 5:24 says, *"And they that are Christ's have crucified the flesh with the affections and lusts. If we live in the Spirit, let us also walk in the Spirit."* This is where the choice comes in. Though the Spirit lives in me, I must make a conscious choice to walk in Him. Every believer either walks in the Spirit or walks in the flesh. If I walk in the flesh, the manifestations of the flesh will come out through my life. If I walk in the Spirit, then the manifestations of the spirit, including the spirit of meekness, will be manifested in my life. As I follow the Spirit through the Word of God, then I can walk in the Spirit and experience and exhibit personal meekness.

Too many Christians have goals other than meekness. They are wrapped up pursuits that distract them from the calling of God to help rescue those ensnared by Satan. Writing to Timothy, Paul said, *"But thou, O man of God, flee these things; and follow after righteousness, godliness, faith, love, patience, meekness."* (1 Timothy 6:11) If we are going to become men and women of consistent meekness, then we must make meekness our lifelong pursuit. There are some things that we should actually run away from them because they are so bad for us. At the same time, there are things we should run toward, and among those traits is meekness. In the last chapter, we talked about how Moses was an example of meekness in action and how that meekness demonstrated when he was subjected to a harsh and unjustified attack from his own family members. The Bible says there was no one else in the whole world who was as meek as Moses. How did he become meek?

If you remember the story of Moses, he was born at a time when every male Hebrew baby was supposed to be killed at birth. Instead, his mother hid him as long as she could and then placed him in a basket in the Nile River, where he was found by Pharaoh's daughter. Moses was reared in the palace, having every advantage available to a member of the royal family. He was educated and trained in all of the sciences and all of the knowledge that was available to a man in Egypt at that time. However, he was visiting with the Hebrews when he saw an Egyptian taskmaster abusing one of them. Moses killed the taskmaster and buried him in the sand. This hardly fits with the quality of meekness. There are many ways to solve a problem, but murder is not recommended. In Stephen's sermon in Acts 7, there is a fascinating commentary about what motivated Moses to murder this man. This was not done in the heat of passion. It was cold and calculated. Moses committed murder because he thought that was the best way to advance the acceptance of his leadership by the Israelites. Acts 7:23-25 says, *"And when he was full forty years old, it came into his heart to visit his brethren the children of Israel."* And *seeing one of them suffer wrong, he defended him, and avenged him that was oppressed, and smote the Egyptian: For he supposed his brethren would have understood how that God by his hand would deliver them:*

but they understood not."

Apparently, at this point Moses knew his mission in life. God had told him that he was to deliver the Hebrew people from Egyptian bondage. Moses intended his action to be a signal to the Israelites of his commitment to help deliver them. He assumed that if he defended the Hebrew and killed the Egyptian, the people would believe "Moses is on our side." (Oftentimes, we make the greatest mistakes in our lives by "supposing.") This is not the spirit of meekness; in fact, it's about as far away from meekness as you can get. There is not a shred of evidence that Moses had any meekness at all at forty years of age, yet when we meet him some forty years later in Numbers 12, God says this is the meekest man on all the face of the earth. What happened during those forty years that changed Moses? This arrogant, self-willed would-be leader of a nation found himself instead the leader of a herd of sheep. The Egyptians hated shepherds—they considered them "an abomination." (Genesis 46:34) Moses once had the hottest chariot with the fastest horse, the newest clothes, and the automatic deference granted by everyone who was a member of the royal family. Now, he is stuck for decades in the dirtiest job he could imagine.

Do you know how God takes us from pride and self will to meekness and humility? He does it by breaking us through trials and pressuring us to do things that we would not do naturally, and if necessary, by humiliating us. In fact, the Old Testament Hebrew word for meekness is the word for humility or humble. Moses was stripped of all these things that had been a source of self confidence and pride. Sheep do not care if you have a Ph.D. or if you were reared in Pharaoh's home. They are just dumb sheep. God used those sheep to teach Moses a lesson in meekness. I have never yet heard anyone say, "I want to be greatly used of God. So, God, I want you to take me and make me do something so incredibly embarrassing and shameful. Make me do a dirty job nobody would ever want to do." We would not ask for that; but God has a way of giving us those tasks, because God is committed to breaking our pride. He is committed to making us empathetic with people and their problems and needs, so we will not be so critical of them; and so that we can with meekness instruct them in the right way.

But, it took more than just sheep to teach Moses meekness. Moses also needed a face to face encounter with God. You know the story of the burning bush when God appeared to Moses and commissioned him to go back to Egypt to lead the children of Israel to freedom. This is what Moses had wanted more than anything else. However, now that the opportunity is presented to him, he balks. He argues with God and lists all the reasons why he is not the right man for the job. God had taken away everything on which Moses relied; now Moses needed to learn that he could rely on God. Only then was he ready to become a truly meek leader for God's people. As we saw earlier, Moses was doing what God wanted in leading the people, but that did not mean they liked it. They were constantly grumbling and complaining about his leadership. They accused him of wanting to kill all of them. They complained that they did not have leeks and onions anymore for their cooking. Through it all, Moses did not retaliate. Instead, he relied on God to defend him.

Because Moses was meek and accepted the will of God, He did

not have to fight and argue about his rights. I do not know where you are today, but I doubt any of us can say that we are totally meek. What is God going to do about it? He will do the same thing He did to Moses. God is going to bring fiery trials into your life…people that you don't like, problems that you would not wish on your worst enemy. Malachi 3:3 says, *"He shall sit as a refiner and purifier of silver."* The trials that come into our lives are designed not for our punishment, but for our purification. I read a wonderful account of a person who went to watch a silversmith. He said, "I made an appointment to watch him at work. I didn't mention anything about the reason for my interest. I had seen this passage in Malachi 3. The only thing the refiner of silver knew was that I was curious about the process of refining silver. I watched the silversmith and saw how he put the piece of silver over the fire and let it heat up. He explained to me that in refining silver, one needed to hold the piece of silver in the middle of the fire where the flames are the hottest in order that they might burn off all the impurities. I thought to myself, 'That is why God holds me in such a hot spot. It is that He might burn off all the impurities.' I then asked the silversmith if it was true that he had to sit there in front of the fire the whole time that the silver was being refined. He told me that not only did he have to sit there holding the silver in the fire, but he has to keep his eyes on the silver at all times while it is in the fire. Then, I asked the silversmith how he knew when the silver was fully refined. He smiled as he told me that when he saw his image in the silver, it was fully refined."

Ralph Waldo Emerson complained about the preacher whose doctrine correct was but there was something sadly missing from his delivery and his message. Every one of us starts out that way, and it is only through the refining fire that God breaks us of our self will and brings us to a place of absolute submission and contentment with whatever He has for our lives. Then, we are free to help people and instruct them with the truths of God's Word in a way that will maximize the possibility of them being motivated to recover themselves out of the snare of the devil. Here is the problem—silver has no legs and no will. It stays in the fire. We have the option of running from God's refining process. We flee the problems and the pressure and refuse to endure the pain that would make us useful and beautiful for His purpose. As a result, we never develop a spirit of meekness, and our ministries are curtailed and short changed. May God help us to endure the trials of the fires that He brings into our lives. I found a beautiful poem that so perfectly expresses God's plan. It is called *The Refiner's Fire.*

There burns a fire with sacred heat,

White hot with holy flame,

And all who dare pass through its blaze

Will not emerge the same.

Some as bronze and some as silver,

Some as gold, and then with great skill

All are hammered by their sufferings

On the anvil of God's will.

The refiner's fire

Has now become my soul's desire.

Purged, cleansed, and purified

That the Lord may be glorified.

He is consuming my soul,

refining me, making me whole.

No matter what I may lose,

I choose the refiner's fire.

I am learning how to trust his touch

To crave the fire's embrace,

For though my past with sin was etched

His mercies did erase.

Each time His purging cleanses deeper,

I'm not sure that I'll survive.

Yet the strength in growing weaker

Keeps my hungry soul alive."

Are you in the fire today? Allow it to produce meekness in your soul, and you will be changed forever. Even more importantly, you will be equipped for a powerful and effective ministry in meekness to those who are ensnared by Satan.

CHAPTER THIRTEEN

THE WAR FOR RECOVERY

"And the servant of the Lord must not strive; but be gentle unto all men, apt to teach, patient, In meekness instructing those that oppose themselves; if God peradventure will give them repentance to the acknowledging of the truth; And that they may recover themselves out of the snare of the devil, who are taken captive by him at his will." (2 Timothy 2:24-26)

We have been focusing on the things that make us effective at helping those who are ensnared; now our text turns to look at the captives. This simple descriptive phrase holds a key to understanding those to whom we minister: "those that oppose themselves." Have you ever looked at someone and wondered, "Why are they doing that? It's destructive, self-defeating, and can't possibly lead to any good end. Why do they keep going down that road?" That person may well be in the snares of Satan, and thus acting in a self-destructive manner, opposing themselves. Other than a person getting saved, I do not know of anything more beautiful than the recovery of a person who has been caught in the snare of the devil. We have the privilege of seeing that over and over again through the ministries of Reformers Unanimous. I want to be very clear on this point though—that never happens without a fight. There is an opposition, both from Satan and from within the person in captivity that must be overcome before freedom can be realized.

Those of us who know Christ and name His name are used to opposition. We understand that there is both internal and external opposition, division, and disagreement to be faced. Friction oftentimes comes into our relationships such as those of a parent/child, husband/wife, employer/employee, neighbor to neighbor, friend to friend, or church member to church member. The "blame game" started in the Garden of Eden when Adam blamed Eve and Eve blamed the serpent, and it has been going strong ever since. However, the conflict and friction Paul is talking about here is not external, but internal. This is vital military intelligence in the campaign to recover those who are ensnared. We cannot successfully fulfill the mission and ministry of the local New Testament church without participating in this crucial task. I want to look at this self opposition and answer four questions about it in order to help prepare you to work with and minister to these people. What is it? Who can get it? What is the cause? How can it be cured?

The Greek word Paul used here by inspiration of the Holy Spirit is a compound word used nowhere else in the entire New Testament. From its usage in secular literature and a study of the two root words, we find that it is a combination of "anti" and "choose" or "decide." The person who opposes himself has a divided mind and cannot make a good decision. He is for it, and he is against it; he wants to go this way, but he wants to go that way too. When someone is opposing himself, he finds it impossible to make and keep commitments in the decisions that he makes. The same word used for decisions is also used to describe covenants and binding legal agreements. When we oppose ourselves, there is a dilemma inside our minds that makes it impossible for us to make that kind of serious commitment. The prophet Amos asked the rhetorical question, *"Can two walk together except they be agreed?"* (Amos 3:3) An external conflict is bad, but an internal conflict is even worse. If you are having a conflict with someone else, then you can get away from them; but if the conflict is inside your own heart and mind, where can you go?

There is a great illustration of this internal conflict in the story of the Old Testament prophet Elijah on top of Mt. Carmel. The false prophets of Baal had arrived for a contest. Each side had a sacrifice on an altar and then prayed to call down fire from heaven. The children of Israel were there to witness the contest and judge which was the true God. After the prophets of Baal tried repeatedly and failed, it was Elijah's turn. He asked the people of Israel a revealing question. *"How long halt ye between two opinions? If the LORD be God, then follow him: but if Baal, then follow him."* (1 Kings 18:21) The word "halt" here does not mean to wait, but rather, it is the Old English word for crippled. The people were crippled because they wanted to follow both God and Baal. By the way, the devil does not mind if you follow God as long as you give him a little bit of room to operate in your life too. If you are trying to follow both, then you will be ensnared before long. The people knew that Jehovah was the true God, but they were not confident that He had their best interests at heart. So, they were trying to cover their bases by adding Baal worship to their religious observance. That indecision crippled them, and led them astray.

What happens when we oppose ourselves? The answer is found the book of James. James 1:8 says, *"A double minded man is unstable in all his ways."* Those who oppose themselves have a pattern of instability about them. They are zigzagging their way through life. All they could do and all they should do and accomplish for God's glory and kingdom is hampered, nullified, and hindered because they could not overcome this double mindedness. Jesus described this in a great illustration in the Sermon on the Mount. He said, *"The light of the body is the eye: if therefore thine eye be single, thy whole body shall be full of light. But if thine eye be evil, thy whole body shall be full of darkness."* (Matthew 6:22-24) Our eyes are designed to work together. Together, they focus to give you good vision. But, what happens if your eyes don't focus? Imagine your left eye looking at one thing while your right looks off in another direction. You would have a hard time seeing anything clearly. My daughter Janelle has this problem. Because of a complication when she was born, the occipital lobe of her brain was deprived of oxygen. That is the part of the brain that controls your vision. As a result, she does not have a "single eye," and everything that is up close to her is blurry.

When you allow yourself to start debating whether or not you are going to do what God says, then you are losing your single focus; and soon, you will find your vision blurred, and you are going to find yourself doing the dumbest things. You cannot even imagine the dumb things you will do when you oppose yourself.

She was a pastor's wife, a woman who knew the Word of God and taught the women in her church about how to love their husbands and honor the Lord. Then, she started talking to a guy in a chat room on the internet. Now, she is leaving her husband and children to move to Texas to be with some man she has never even met. Is that smart? No, it's blindness and folly. It all started when she allowed herself to debate whether or not she was going to do what God told her to do. What happened? She opened herself up to the snares of the devil. She lost her single eye. Her focus was gone and tragedy followed.

In Matthew 12:25, Jesus said, *"Every kingdom divided against itself is brought to desolation."* What is true of a kingdom is true of an individual as well. You cannot successfully live in a divided way. If we lose our unity, if we lose our single eye, if we allow ourselves to debate if we should go in this direction or that, then we are on our way to self-destruction. This leads to personal frustration. We tend to think of the Apostle Paul as a super Christian. Indeed, he accomplished much for the kingdom of God. But, he faced the same frustrations and struggles that we do. In a remarkably candid and transparent statement, Paul described the battle that went on in his life. *"For we know that the law is spiritual: but I am carnal, sold under sin. For that which I do I allow not: for what I would, that do I not; but what I hate, that do I. Now if I do that I would not, it is no more I that do it, but sin that dwelleth in me. But I see another law in my members, warring against the law of my mind, and bringing me into captivity to the law of sin which is in my members. O wretched man that I am! who shall deliver me from the body of this death?"* (Romans 7:14&15, 20, 23&24)

Paul was in a bad spot. I am so glad that the passage does not end like that. Yes, Paul had problems and struggles, but there is an answer, a cure for self opposition—spiritual maturity.

When you read these words from Paul, just a few verses after his expression of frustration, it almost sounds like it was written by an entirely different person. In a sense, it is (although we know that each word was given by inspiration of the Holy Spirit), for now Paul is talking not as a man struggling with self opposition but as a man walking in victory. *"There is therefore now no condemnation to them which are in Christ Jesus, who walk not after the flesh, but after the Spirit. For the law of the Spirit of life in Christ Jesus hath made me free from the law of sin and death."* (Romans 8:1&2)

When we get our minds in line with God's will and God's Spirit who is indwelling us, and when our thinking is spiritually minded, then we are in cooperation with God; and there is an internal peace and harmony that is indescribably wonderful. Where there is peace inside your heart and mind because you know you are pleasing Him, you know that you are protected from the vulnerability that would come from indecision and double-mindedness. Paul uses the word 'law' here not as a reference specifically to the Old Testament law but to a natural law. If you paid attention in science class, you learned about Sir Isaac Newton. In addition to being a brilliant mathematician and physicist, he was also a devoted Christian. Some say that a falling apple instigated his intense interest in studying what became known as the law of gravity. The law of gravity, simply stated, is that "what goes up must come down." If I jump up, I am not going to continue up until I hit the ceiling, I am going to come back down.

That is the law of gravity at work. Gravity is what keeps us on terra firma. However, the law of gravity can be overcome by another law.

The 747 jumbo jet is a monstrosity. It is 231 feet and 6 inches long and has a 211 foot 3-inch wingspan. Fully loaded, with 60,000 gallons of fuel, it can fly over 7000 miles at 35,000 feet at a speed of 570 mph. It weighs 950,000 pounds. How can that big monstrosity get up off the ground? It uses another law, Bernoulli's law. The law of Bernoulli properly applied can overcome the law of gravity, so that something can be done that is otherwise humanly impossible.

I have good news for you. The law of sin and death that is on all of us can be overcome by a greater law, the law of the Spirit of life. When you and I walk in obedience to God, wholeheartedly, not opposing ourselves or being double minded but yielding ourselves to Him, we can soar above the sin that has been holding us down. We have been talking about rescuing others, but allow me talk to you about you personally for a moment.

Are you in an internal struggle, having yielded to certain things you know are against God's plan and will? Are you allowing them into your mind and defending them, perhaps by comparison to others? Do you say, "I'm so dedicated in all these other areas." or "When I look around, I'm better than most people." You can argue yourself into remaining disobedient to God, but what a frustrating way to live life. While you are in the snare, the real purpose for your life, the reason for your being here is rendered ineffective; because when you are in the snare, you cannot be out doing the things that God called you to do.

If that is you today, a great place to start is for you to personally yield to God and ask for His help. Most of us know the issue. We need to say that it is no longer up for debate. We should admit that we are wrong and God is right, and we are not going to fight against it any longer. I beg of you, do not think that this cannot happen to you. Do not ignore the warning signs. Take personal responsibility to be a servant of the Lord. Follow the Spirit of God and walk according to His guidance, so that you can not only be free yourself, but you can also help others recover themselves from the snare of the devil.

CHAPTER FOURTEEN

REPENTANCE AND RECOVERY (PART ONE)

"And the servant of the Lord must not strive; but be gentle unto all men,
apt to teach, patient, In meekness instructing those that oppose themselves;
if God peradventure will give them repentance to the acknowledging of
the truth; And that they may recover themselves out of the snare of the
devil, who are taken captive by him at his will." (2 Timothy 2:24-26)

On June 24, 1859, a Swiss banker named Jean-Henri Dunant was in Italy to discuss problems with trade due to the war that was sweeping across Europe. He came upon the battlefield at Solefrino where one of the most brutal battles of the Austro-Sardian War was taking place. When the fighting stopped, some 6,000 soldiers were dead and as many as 40,000 more were injured. Dunant realized with horror that the screams of pain and cries for help that he heard were going unanswered. There were no organized efforts to care for them. Their own armies abandoned them. The injured men who could still move dragged themselves into town and begged for help. For three days and three nights, Jean-

Henri Dunant worked feverishly to help as many of those men as he could. He insisted that the townspeople treat wounded soldiers from both armies equally. When he returned home, Dunant abandoned his banking career and began urging the creation of a new group to care for the aid of injured soldiers, regardless of their nationality. Out of his vision came the organization we know today as the Red Cross.

Today, another war is taking place, a spiritual battle in which the devil is doing everything he can to not just wound but capture people and take them prisoner. Temptation and Satanic influence has grown exponentially in my generation. In the last chapter, we saw the danger of opposing ourselves, and how it can lead to a snare. Now, we see that if those who are ensnared are to be freed, they must repent, that is they must change their mind. No one ever does better until he first thinks better. No one consistently does right unless he is thinking right. Thinking differently is essential to recovering from Satan's snares. Satan is a deceiver, and he has been from the beginning. He is dishonest. He is the father of lies (John 8:44), and he has birthed many, many children in this world that spout his lies. Many Christians begin to debate Satan's lies versus God's truth and soon find themselves in a snare of the devil because they come to believe the lie. If we allow him to make us doubt the truth and distort the truth, eventually we will deny the truth and disobey the truth. Eve should never have debated God's words with the devil; but she did, and it ended in death.

In the 6,000 years that have passed since the Garden of Eden, the devil has honed his skills of deception. He is very, very good at taking people who have it made and bringing them to a place of choosing to disobey the One who created them and gave them such wonderful blessings. Without God, they would not even exist, let alone enjoy all the good things in their lives. Yet, the devil turns their minds and persuades them to begin debating within their own thoughts. When the devil wants to engage you or me in a debate, I would suggest we send Jesus to the door. We need to disassociate ourselves from everything the devil brings our way. Repentance is necessary because the devil is a deceiver, and he attempts to change the way we think about God, about the Bible, and about obedience to Christ. When he succeeds in changing our thinking, we need God to change it back.

The second reason that repentance is necessary for anyone being recovered out of the snare of the devil is because of the process that occurs. The decisions that we make as a result of debating with the devil lead to a direction in our lives. The direction of our lives leads to a destination, and that is usually not a destination that we intended to reach. Think about the consequences of Adam's sin. He was cast out of his beautiful home in the perfect Garden of Eden. Now, he had to earn his food by the sweat of his brow. Now, his children would have a sin nature; and one day, his first son would kill his second son in a jealous rage. Listening to Satan's lies took him much further than he could ever have anticipated. It is very hard to convince someone in the early stages of sin of this truth. The Bible says that there is pleasure in sin for a season. (Hebrews 11:25) As long as you are in that pleasurable season, anyone who is trying to rescue you will be hard-pressed to convince you to think otherwise.

The devil promises freedom, but he only delivers slavery. It would be better to reconsider at the beginning before you plunge deeper and deeper into sin and away from God and destruction becomes epidemic in your life. It would be better to stop before the consequences become irreversible. But, that will only happen if we repent and change our thinking. Once we start listening to the debate of the devil and begin to doubt God and His goodness that He has the best in mind for us, we are on our way to slavery. All of us are vulnerable. Just because I have been saved for over fifty years and have been in church almost every week of my life, just because I have spent years teaching people the truths of the Bible, does not mean I am not just as vulnerable as anyone else. I saw right living modeled in my family. I had a godly mom and dad and a good family upbringing. But, the devil could still snare me. The battle is won or lost day by day in my mind, just as it is in yours.

If we have made bad decisions and need to repent, what do we do? Or, if we are working with someone who is ensnared, how can we help? How can our mind be changed? How can we help to influence people to change their minds? A change in our way of thinking demands consistent, concentrated influence from that which is true. I tell people who visit our church, "If you come to our church, I'm going to tell you the truth. I'm going to preach the Word of God. As long as I stay with the Bible, you can have absolute confidence that I'm telling you the truth." Repentance requires a consistent and concentrated diet of the truth. It was no mistake that when John the Baptist appeared on the scene, he preached a message of repentance. Bible preaching and Bible teaching is designed to lead people to change the way they are thinking. We need to be brought back into line, to focus on truth by coming regularly to the Bible and the preaching and teaching of the Book. That input will bring us back into the realization of what is true, what is right, what is good, and what has eternal value and purpose. That is the purpose of preaching and teaching the Word.

One of the main reasons that so many Christians today are confused and doubting God's Word and denying God's Word and finding themselves in the snares of the devil is the devaluation of preaching and teaching the Bible. In far too many places, entertainment has become the focus of the church. Sadly, this is not just true in false churches and liberal denominations. Many churches that once stood solidly for the fundamentals of the faith have left behind their previous convictions and replaced the "two-edged sword" with something less demanding. The Bible is God's opinion on those matters that are important in life. We need a steady diet of consistently knowing what God thinks about things. But simply going to a good church once a week, twice, or even three times, as valuable as that is, it is not enough. You and I need to take the Bible each morning and study it for ourselves. We need to immerse our minds in the Truth.

Second Timothy 3:16 says, "*All scripture is given by inspiration of God, and is profitable for doctrine,*" (that is teaching us what is right) "*for reproof,*" (that is teaching us what is wrong) "*for correction,*" (that is teaching us when we're wrong and how to get right) "*for instruction in righteousness.*" (That is how to stay right.) We want to change the way that we are thinking; because when we get our mind in line with the Bible, when we are thinking with the mind of Christ, we will repent and be set free. That should be the focus of the church—to bring people's minds in line with the Word of God. I shudder when I hear people say something like, "I just don't get what I used to get out of church anymore. Maybe I need to find somewhere else. Somewhere they aren't so strict, maybe somewhere that they don't preach the Bible all the time, someplace that will make me feel good." That is such a danger sign. The Bible is not bad news, it is good news. That is what the word "gospel" means. I think the Bible should be preached and taught positively. But, we do not need a different message. We do not have to be left wondering what is right and what is wrong. We do not have to debate these things. We just need to find out what God has to say and do that. It will bring us to repentance and freedom.

Paul told the Philippians how to change their thinking. He wrote, "*Finally, brethren, whatsoever things are true, whatsoever things are honest, whatsoever things are just, whatsoever things are pure, whatsoever things are lovely, whatsoever things are of good report; if there be any virtue, and if there be any praise, think on these things.*" (Philippians 4:8) Right-thinking leads to the right direction in life; and the right direction in life leads to the right destination. This is not easy, but I am not sure where we got the idea that it was supposed to be easy. We are in a war. We have a determined and dedicated foe. He is out to destroy and enslave us. If you do not allow him to control your thinking, you will be spared many of the problems in life. If you do, stop and change things before it is too late. How can we repent? How can we change the way that someone thinks? We must put a stop to every untruthful influence in our lives. If it is not true, if it is not honest, it is not just, if it does not fit within the parameters of God's Word, and you have an ability to turn it off and keep it from influencing you in any way, then you must make that decision. You must decide, "I am not going to entertain a lie."

This issue defines the struggle that we are having in Christianity today. Even in good churches and Christian homes, we are allowing "a little leaven," and it is leavening the whole lump just as the Bible said it would. (Galatians 5:9) It does not take very much of a lie to undo a whole truth. Specifically, what do you watch? If you watch lies, and consider them, it opens your mind up to debate. Usually, when lies are presented, they are presented in the guise of something beneficial, something that is good, something that is wholesome, something that is fun. So, we indulge them. Eventually, because we have diluted the truth, we find ourselves in a snare. Oftentimes, this is why people who live a very sheltered childhood, tend to think better. If you seek to eliminate any of the influences of the devil on your life and fill your life with consistent, concentrated truth from God's Word, then you maximize the possibility of keeping a good mind that will lead to the right direction which will in turn lead to the right destination for your life. Heed this solemn warning from Solomon. He wrote, *"Cease, my son, to hear the instruction that causeth to err from the words of knowledge."* (Proverbs 19:27)

We cannot live in complete isolation. We are to be in the world, but not of the world. (John 17:14-16) There are going to be occasions in our life when we may not be able to turn that voice off. It might be an employer who says things that would lead us astray. You may have to listen, but you do not have to let that dominate and change your thinking. The problem comes when we knowingly allow those voices through friendships or entertainment to promote a lie, and we open ourselves up to becoming snared by the devil. Reject that thinking and those voices. Without this kind of personal commitment, you will never repent. How much truth are you getting during the hours of the week? Are there any untruths that you are subjected to voluntarily? What should you do about it? Turn it off! Excuse yourself! Stay with the truth and with people who believe the truth and let the truth change the way that you think.

CHAPTER FIFTEEN

REPENTANCE AND RECOVERY (PART TWO)

"And the servant of the Lord must not strive; but be gentle unto all men, apt to teach, patient, In meekness instructing those that oppose themselves; if God peradventure will give them repentance to the acknowledging of the truth; And that they may recover themselves out of the snare of the devil, who are taken captive by him at his will." (2 Timothy 2:24-26)

A s we continue to look at what it means to repent, particularly as it relates to our efforts to help in recovering people who have been ensnared by Satan, I want to call your attention further to this concept of change. Jesus taught in parables; and often, the disciples failed to grasp what He was teaching. We see one of these instances when, as so often happened, it was Peter who spoke up to Jesus for an explanation. Jesus did not respond with soothing words; in fact, He chastised the disciples for their lack of understanding. *"And Jesus said, Are ye also yet without understanding? Do not ye yet understand, that whatsoever entereth in at the mouth goeth into the belly, and is cast out into the draught?"*(Matthew 15:16&17) This rebuke for a lack of understanding highlights an important truth about repentance. Repentance is not me simply changing my mind; it is God changing my understanding. The only way we repent is when God opens our eyes for us to see and grasp the truth. This is true in salvation; it is true of recovery from snares as well. Paul says it plainly—God gives repentance.

When we receive what God says and we grasp the meaning of it, then and only then has true repentance taken place. Repentance is a change in our understanding which God enacts. When that understanding comes to you, it is not because you are smarter than somebody else; it because God gave repentance. I do the very best I can when I stand to teach or preach from the Word of God. I study and prepare and try to learn all I can; so that I can, in turn, impart those truths to those who hear. I can tell someone what the Bible says and try to make it clear and plain, but I cannot give anyone spiritual understanding. Only the Spirit of God does that. When are listening to teaching, we have a responsibility to focus and pay attention. Paul pointed this out to Timothy when he wrote, *"Consider what I say."* (2 Timothy 2:7) Unless we work at it, we will find our minds drifting away from what is being taught.

We do not encourage people to check their brains at the door when they come to our church. We are not about using emotional appeals to coerce or compel people to respond. Our approach is to give people the Word of God in a way that maximizes the possibility that people will listen and then rely on the Holy Spirit to do the work in the hearts and minds of those who hear. It all comes down to Him. Paul not only told Timothy to pay attention, he also said,

"And the Lord give thee understanding in all things." (2 Timothy 2:7) Spiritual truths can only be understood spiritually. Paul was consistent—he did not just think getting understanding from God was for Timothy, he thought the same thing about himself. *"For this cause I Paul, the prisoner of Jesus Christ for you Gentiles, If ye have heard of the dispensation of the grace of God which is given me to youward: How that by revelation he made known unto me the mystery; (as I wrote afore in few words, Whereby, when ye read, ye may understand my knowledge in the mystery of Christ) Which in other ages was not made known unto the sons of men, as it is now revealed unto his holy apostles and prophets by the Spirit."* (Ephesians 3:1-5)

Paul had a great education. He studied at the finest schools, he spoke several languages, and he was well versed in the classics and the knowledge of the day. That is not what he credited for his understanding of the mysteries of God—he understood them by revelation.

That is how repentance works. Repentance is when God helps us to understand a truth out of His Word that changes the way we think and the way that we live our lives. There may be a great many things in the Bible that do not make any sense to you. There is probably going to be some things in Scripture that will never make sense to you this side of eternity. That is not a bad thing. If we could understand everything there is to know about God, then that would be a dangerous thing. There are mysteries that we may not understand, but there are also truths in the Bible that we can understand. We understand them not because they are easily known, and not because we study the Bible more than others, or not because we are smarter than somebody else. But, the truths are understood because God opens our minds to understanding. Often, we fall into the trap of equating knowledge with understanding, but the two are not the same. The devil knows the Bible and quoted the Scriptures when tempting Christ, but he has no spiritual understanding.

First Corinthians 2:7&8 says, *"But we speak the wisdom of God in a mystery, even the hidden wisdom, which God ordained before the world unto our glory: Which none of the princes of this world knew: for had they known it, they would not have crucified the Lord of glory."* God clouded his mind concerning these mysteries so that He could move His plan right under the very nose of the devil and his demons. They had no idea what God was doing and became unwitting instruments of His will. He does not reveal His purpose to the devil, but He will reveal those truths and mysteries to you. It is no surprise that God insists on being the One who opens our understanding. He will not share His glory with anyone. We only receive repentance—that moment when the light comes on and we "get it"—from Him. Repentance produces a change in our thinking and then a change in our living.

It was a special understanding of the Scriptures that equipped the disciples to become the apostles and lead the early church. After His resurrection, Jesus appeared to them to prepare them for what was to come. *"And he said unto them, These are the words which I spake unto you, while I was yet with you, that all things must be fulfilled, which were written in the law of Moses, and in the prophets, and in the psalms, concerning me. Then opened he their understanding, that they might understand the scriptures."* (Luke 24:44&45) Up to that time, people had not been able to understand how Christ could be so mercilessly and cruelly mistreated. There are prophecies throughout the Old Testament concerning the crucifixion, but their knowledge had not yet led to understanding. Even after Jesus told them He would be crucified, they still did not understand. They had walked with Jesus for more than three years; but until He opened their understanding, they had none.

I am of the opinion that we need a good dose of repentance and understanding in our churches and our lives. We have too many Christians messing around in the world and debating whether or not they are going to follow Christ. They have allowed Satan to distort their lives and many are being destroyed; yet they sit back and say, "I don't understand. This doesn't make sense to me." We need the Lord to give us understanding. Intellect, or mere exposure to the Scriptures, will not guarantee an understanding of the truths of the Bible. There was no people better versed in the Scriptures than the Pharisees and the Scribes, yet over and over again Jesus said, "Neither do they understand; neither do they understand." Everything we can do is not enough. The Bible says that Judas Iscariot repented after he betrayed Jesus, but it was not the right kind of repentance.

Matthew 27:3 says, *"Then Judas, which had betrayed him, when he saw that he was condemned, repented himself, and brought again the thirty pieces of silver to the chief priests and elders."*

Notice that he repented himself. This is not the repentance that God grants which actually brings change. This kind of repentance is a change of mind that does not result in a change in heart or actions.

It is possible for us to say the words on our own, "I have repented. I changed my mind about that." Are you sure? Is your repentance a result of God divinely granting you a change in understanding that then leads to a change in decision-making that leads to a change in direction, which ultimately leads to a change in destiny in your life? This is the repentance that saves. This is the repentance that sanctifies. This is the repentance that recovers one out of the snare of the devil. It is not about us and does not depend on us; it is all about God. Are you experiencing biblical repentance? Are you experiencing a change in your understanding? At times in my life, I can remember sitting in church and thinking, "I don't know how these people could be so interested because I can't make any sense out of this." Later, after I came to the point in my life where God brought me to repentance, I was amazed at how smart my pastor had grown in that short period of time. I do not take for granted the wonderful mercy of God in opening the eyes of my understanding, that I might see the necessity of change in my thinking, so that He could also change the way that I live. That is the meaning of God granting us repentance.

CHAPTER SIXTEEN

UNDERSTANDING THE KEY OF KNOWLEDGE

"And the servant of the Lord must not strive; but be gentle unto all men, apt to teach, patient, In meekness instructing those that oppose themselves; if God peradventure will give them repentance to the acknowledging of the truth; And that they may recover themselves out of the snare of the devil, who are taken captive by him at his will." (2 Timothy 2:24-26)

I heard somebody say, "Truth is not absolute. Truth is relative." When he was asked if he was certain he said, "Absolutely!" That was a funny response, but the truth is no laughing matter. From the temptation of Eve in the Garden of Eden to this very day, there has been a focused effort to lead people to believe that truth is not absolute, that it is not identifiable; but it is not reliable, and that it changes. That deception continues to be used by our enemy because it continues to work. In fact, surveys show that a majority of people who claim to be Christians do not believe there is any such thing as absolute truth that applies at all times in all circumstances. Now, I am sure that not all of those people are really believers, but it is a frightening reminder of how successful Satan has been at snaring people with the lie of relativity. The Bible teaches contrary to that. The truth is absolute and unchanging.

In contrast to Satan's lies, Jesus came and proclaimed truth. He taught that truth could be known. In John 8:32, Jesus said, *"And ye shall know the truth, and the truth shall make you free."* He taught that He was truth. In John 14:6, Jesus said, *"I am the way, the truth and the life."* He taught that God's Word was truth. In John 17:17, Jesus said, *"Sanctify them through thy truth: thy word is truth."* Truth can be found within the confines of the Word of God, the Scriptures, and the Bible. Every attack by Satan against truth is ultimately an attack against the Bible. If the Bible is not authentic, then it will not be authoritative in our lives. Sadly, the devil has been very successful at getting our society and even our churches to a position where the Bible as truth is not as widely accepted as it once was. Jesus said, *"Ye are of your father the devil, and the lusts of your father ye will do. He was a murderer from the beginning. When he speaketh a lie, he speaketh of his own: for he is a liar, and the father of it. And because I tell you the truth, ye believe me not."* (John 8:44&45) What was the Devil murdering at the beginning? He was murdering the truth. That is what, "Yea hath God said?" was all about. People who are in the snare of the devil and have been taken captive by him have had their minds warped. They are not even certain what is true and what is not true.

The authenticity and accuracy of God's Word has been attacked throughout history. One of the most effective of those attacks was launched by Charles Darwin. Though people tend to describe evolution as a secular philosophy, in fact, it is just as much a religious belief system as Christianity is. It depends on faith, not in God, but in a magic process of billions and billions of years to work changes that produced the world we see today. Darwinism has been one of the greatest contributors to doubt and denial of the truth of God's Word because it runs completely contrary to Scripture. If truth is man centered, if there is no God, if there is no Creator, if there is no author and finisher, if there is no judge, then man becomes his own authority and truth becomes relative. There are no longer any absolutes, and any form of behavior can be justified.

This casual attitude toward truth has also infiltrated into the church. Recently, I was reading some literature about small group Bible discussions. It was written by an evangelical writer—not some heathen philosopher. Yet, in the recommendations for how you should structure these group Bible discussions, he suggested that when you are teaching the lesson, you should simply read a portion of Scripture, and then go around the room and ask your students, "What does this mean to you?" I think his purpose was good in that he wanted to get the young people involved rather than destroying their faith, but that is a horribly wrong approach. The Bible means what it says, not what I think it means. Does the truth change according to how I feel about it? No, it does not. We should boldly and confidently explain and apply what the Bible says and declare it as truth. We need to leave no room for doubt about the unchanging and eternal nature of the truth.

This was the hallmark of Jesus' teaching. The thing that impressed the people was that Jesus, *"taught as one having authority."* (Matthew 7:29) In other words, He spoke as one who was confident in the authority of the Scriptures that He used and taught. He did not use them tentatively. He did not teach people something and then ask what it meant to them. He did not say, "Well, the Old Testament was written centuries ago, and it doesn't apply to our modern world." The truth never changes. The Word never changes. God never changes. Yet, I continue to hear statements like, "I know what the Bible says, but we live in a different society." That is the road to being ensnared and enslaved. Once truth becomes relative, you are unable to have stability and freedom in your life.

Despite the claims many people are making today and the devil is working overtime to promote, truth can be known. And, truth is worth defending. For many generations, Christians died for the sake of truth even though they could have saved their lives by compromise. If we had that kind of persecution in our country today, I am not sure how many people who claim the name of Christ would be willing to die rather than adjust their beliefs. Already, most Christians never witness because they are afraid of what someone might say about them. I heard somebody say the other day, "We have too many Secret Service Christians." The truth is not to be hidden; it is to be proclaimed loudly and from the rooftops. I do not care if people call me a religious fanatic; I am going to stand with the truth.

John, the beloved disciple, was the last of the apostles to die. Before he died in exile on Patmos, John trained two men to carry on the work. Their names were Ignatius and Polycarp. For many years, they were leaders of the church. Under the Roman Emperor Trajan, a great persecution arose. Ignatius was taken to Rome and had an audience before Trajan. The Roman ruler offered to spare his life if Ignatius would offer a sacrifice to the Roman gods in public demonstration of his loyalty to the empire. Ignatius refused because truth to him was not negotiable. He was taken into the Coliseum and thrown into the arena with starving wild beasts in front of a sold-out crowd of pagan people who got their entertainment from watching people killed. Polycarp was ordered to curse Christ, but he refused. He was taken into a stadium in front of a bloodthirsty mob. Before his execution, he said, "Eighty-six years I have served Him, and He has never once wronged me. How then shall I blaspheme my King who has saved me?" They burned Polycarp at the stake in that very spot. Truth is worth fighting for; truth is also worth dying for.

I was talking to a woman on a plane a while back. She was being very sincere when she asked me questions. She saw I was reading my Bible, and she struck up a conversation. I had a great opportunity to speak with her. She disbelieved everything I said. She said to me, "That it is all right for you if you need that for something to make you feel better, but I choose not to believe that." I replied to her, "You can choose to not believe that or to believe that, but that doesn't change whether or not it is true. It is true whether you believe it or not. Furthermore, there will be a day when you do believe it." The devil loves it when people think truth depends on them rather than on God and His Word. He has those people ensnared, and they do not even know it.

That spirit of compromise of the truth is infiltrating the church today, especially the movement called the "emergent church." Prolific authors like Tony Jones and Brian McLaren have written books selling millions of copies. Leaders are reading their words and being persuaded that truth is relative. Tony Jones wrote, "We do not think that our movement is about changing your worship service. We do not think this is about how you structure your church staff. This is actually about changing your theology. This is about our belief that theology must change to keep up with society. The message is that not only the method must change, but the message must change." Brian McLaren wrote, "I must add that I do not believe that making disciples must equal making adherents to the Christian religion. It may be advisable in many circumstances to make people followers of Jesus and yet remain within their Buddhist, Hindu, or Jewish context."

In his book, *A Heretic's Guide to Eternity*, Spencer Burke wrote, "I'm not sure that I believe in God exclusively as a person anymore. I now incorporate a pantheistic view which is basically that God is all and in all along beside my credo view of God as Father, Son, and Holy Spirit." Doug Pagitt in an interview said, "God is going to judge the life and repair, restore, and heal the life of everybody in the same way." Rob Bell wrote a best-selling book called *Love Wins*. He says, "A staggering number of people have been taught that a select few called Christians will spend forever in a peaceful, joyous place called Heaven, while the rest of humanity spends forever in torment and punishment in Hell with no chance for anything better. This is misguided, toxic, and it ultimately subverts the contagious spread of Jesus' message of love, peace, and forgiveness that the world desperately needs to hear." In his book, *A Generous Orthodoxy*, Bell says, "Ask me if Christianity, my version of it, your version of it, the pope's version, whoever's is orthodox, meaning true and here is my honest answer: It's true, a little but not yet. To be a Christian in a generously orthodox way is not to claim to have the truth captured, stuffed, and mounted on the wall. We are still seeking."

These are the people who are influencing the church to abandon the truth. I am not seeking the truth; I know where it is. I want to learn more about it and understand it better, but it is found within the pages of my King James Bible that God's people have been using for 400 years. I do not have a single doubt about the truth of the Word of God. Rob Bell also said this, "The Christian faith is mysterious to the core. It's about things that ultimately cannot be put into words. Language fails. If we do definitely put God into words, we have at that very moment made God something that God is not." That attitude does away with preaching and teaching the Word. Why bother if I am not able to put God and truth into words? For that matter, why did God bother to give us a Bible at all if words do not convey the truth? In a ridiculous attempt to sound deep and be thought of as intellectual, many are abandoning the clear and simple doctrines of Scripture.

Is it any wonder that there is very little authoritative Bible preaching in the pulpits of our churches today? This leads to doubt and confusion on the part of people. Can you imagine if natural law was not absolute but relative? What would you do if at certain times the law of gravity was active, and at other times it was not? You might get up tomorrow morning and already be up, you would never know. Everything about God's nature and character speaks to absolutes. Whether or not I see the sun come up in the morning, it will come up in the east, and it will set in the west. How could I have figured that out? The answer is because God's laws are absolute, and the church is supposed to be foundation of taking this vital doctrine to the world. First Timothy 3:15 says, *"But if I tarry long, that thou mayest know how thou oughtest to behave thyself in the house of God, which is the church of the living God, the pillar and ground of the truth."* The pillar and ground is what holds the building together. What happens when the church loses its bearings? What happens when it loses its commitment to the Bible being absolutely true? Everything falls apart—not just the church, but society as well.

A missionary friend called me for advice the other day. His sending church has a new pastor. He has changed their Bible to a modern translation, changed the church constitution to avoid taking a stand against drinking alcohol, and they've done it all in the name of grace. When you plant seeds of doubt and begin to question and deny what is in the Bible and what it means, and when you begin teaching that, the church begins to think, how can we be judgmental? Once you open the door and truth becomes relative, you are left with nothing on which to stand. If there are no absolute truths, there is no truth to be acknowledged to lead to escaping the snares of the devil. We must have an absolute Bible. We must have a standard by which we can judge our life and actions. God wants us to be like the believers at Berea in Acts 17, who *"were more noble than those at Thessalonica in that they searched the Scriptures daily whether those things were so."* The Bible is our absolute truth book by which we can make proper decisions in life. It is reliable. It is why we need to study; to rightly divide it.

There will always be those who will deny the truth; those who will seek to dissuade us from obedience to the truth, but that leads to the path to slavery and snares. The only people who have true freedom are those who submit themselves to living by the absolute truths of the Word of God. The devil will promise you freedom; but he is a liar, and he will not deliver on that promise. You will become ensnared and caught in the trap of the devil if you began to doubt, deny, and depart from the absolute truths of the Word of God. There are more than 140 references in the Bible, both in the Old and New Testaments, which describe God's Word as truth. Not one verse casts any doubt on the accuracy, authenticity, and authority of the Scriptures. Not one promise has failed; not one statement has been proven false. You can fully rely on everything the Bible says. It is truth – absolute truth.

God does not give suggestions; He gives commandments. Did you know that a commandment is not the same as a good idea? There is a lot of teaching and preaching today that is a result of people afraid to take a stand. "I would like to make a suggestion to you." No, I do not want to make a suggestion to you. You do not need my opinion. It does not matter what I think. It does not matter what you think either. What matters is what God thinks. What does He say? If we can pull out straight teaching from the Scripture and compare Scripture with Scripture, rightly dividing it, then we can know how we ought to order ourselves. Too many people today are trying to find a new Bible that is "easier" to understand. Instead, we need to stick to the old Book. Get yourself a copy of Webster's 1828 Dictionary, and read the book. The same Holy Spirit of God who inspired the words of Scripture dwells in your heart, and He *will guide you into all truth.*" (John 16:13) We do not need to change the Word to match our ideas; we need to change our ideas to match the Word. Let God's truth be the standard rather than what you think. It will keep you free and help you recover others from the snares of Satan.

CHAPTER SEVENTEEN

USE THE KEY OF KNOWLEDGE

"And the servant of the Lord must not strive; but be gentle unto all men, apt to teach, patient, In meekness instructing those that oppose themselves; if God peradventure will give them repentance to the acknowledging of the truth; And that they may recover themselves out of the snare of the devil, who are taken captive by him at his will." (2 Timothy 2:24-26)

In Luke chapter 11, we see a confrontation between Jesus and a group of lawyers. These were not legal experts as we think of lawyers today, but rather men who were experts in the law of God. They spent their entire lives in the study of the Old Testament. But, despite their great knowledge, they had a very serious problem. Jesus said, *"Woe unto you, lawyers! for ye have taken away the key of knowledge: ye entered not in yourselves, and them that were entering in ye hindered."* (Luke 11:52) There is a vast difference between knowing the truth and acknowledging the truth. Although we must know the truth in order to acknowledge the truth, we may know the truth and yet not acknowledge the truth. It is terrible not to know the truth.

There are many people in the world today who have no Bible. But, I think it is even worse to know the truth but not live it. The Bible is like a key. Jesus spoke to the lawyers and rebuked them for not applying what they knew about the Bible. The Bible is the truth; it is the book of knowledge. Knowing is incredibly important. You cannot acknowledge truth; you cannot come to the truth, without first knowing.

"This know also, that in the last days perilous times shall come. For men shall be lovers of their own selves, covetous, boasters, proud, blasphemers, disobedient to parents, unthankful, unholy, Without natural affection, trucebreakers, false accusers, incontinent, fierce, despisers of those that are good, Traitors, heady, highminded, lovers of pleasures more than lovers of God; Having a form of godliness, but denying the power thereof: from such turn away. For of this sort are they which creep into houses, and lead captive silly women laden with sins, led away with divers lusts, Ever learning, and never able to come to the knowledge of the truth." (2 Timothy 3:1-7) This passage from Paul to Timothy depicts the plight of the lawyers Jesus rebuked perfectly. They were continually learning without ever coming to meaning and applied knowledge. The Bible describes us when we first get saved as babies. The milk that we need to grow up is the Word of God. It is perfectly fine not to have knowledge when you start, but don't stay there. Knowing Christ and knowing His Word is the key. But remember, simply having a key is not enough; you also have to use that key to open the door.

You can study knowledge, and you can study the key. You can learn about all the different things about the key, but that will still not unlock the door. Jesus said the lawyers had taken away the key of knowledge, and that they had not entered in themselves. When we get to know God and we get to know His Word, but we do not take the next step of acknowledging His truth, we fall short. The door of opportunity is opened only when we take the knowledge that we have learned from the Word of God and use it. The Bible is filled with information about all areas of life. The Bible teaches us how to be good parents, good spouses, good employees, good Christians, and more. But, knowing what it says in those areas does not change us; using the key and acknowledging the truth changes us. Understand that acknowledging the truth is not just giving a nod to it and saying, "That's true." Acknowledging is coming into agreement with the truth. It is when we say, "That's true, and I'm going to use the key and unlock it. I'm going to believe what God says in His Word, and I'm going to implement it into my life."

When we take that step and use the key, God unlocks the door to our prison. No matter how much we may want to, we cannot use the truth of the Bible as a key for someone else. You can give people the key and try to help them, but they must turn the key in their own life. If they do not, then they are placing themselves in great danger. Paul described a group of people like that and explained where they ended up. *"Wherefore God also gave them up to uncleanness through the lusts of their own hearts, to dishonour their own bodies between themselves: Who changed the truth of God into a lie, and worshipped and served the creature more than the Creator, who is blessed for ever. Amen. For this cause God gave them up unto vile affections: for even their women did change the natural use into that which is against nature: And likewise also the men, leaving the natural use of the woman, burned in their lust one toward another; men with men working that which is unseemly, and receiving in themselves that recompence of their error which was meet. And even as they did not like to retain God in their knowledge, God gave them over to a reprobate mind, to do those things which are not convenient; Being filled with all unrighteousness, fornication, wickedness, covetousness, maliciousness; full of envy, murder, debate, deceit, malignity; whisperers, Backbiters, haters of God, despiteful, proud, boasters, inventors of evil things, disobedient to parents, Without understanding, covenantbreakers, without natural affection, implacable, unmerciful: Who knowing the judgment of God, that they which commit such things are worthy of death, not only do the same, but have pleasure in them that do them.*" (Romans 1:24-32)

Truth sets us free, but truth we do not apply to our lives takes us deeper into bondage to Satan. The consequences of knowing God but refusing to acknowledge Him are catastrophic. This is true for both individuals and nations. The longer we refuse to act on what we know is true, the deeper into bondage we plunge. This passage of Scripture identifies in graphic detail the end results of failing to turn the key. Romans 1:18 tells us about those who *"hold the truth in unrighteousness."* That literally means to suppress or hold the truth down. If you know the truth but do not act on it, you are headed for perilous times. When Jesus sent out the disciples to preach the Gospel, He told them that some people would refuse to hear the truth, and then He issued a solemn warning. *"Verily I say unto you, It shall be more tolerable for the land of Sodom and Gomorrha in the day of judgment, than for that city.*" (Matthew 10:15) Do not pass by that statement too quickly. The people in Sodom and Gomorrah were wicked and went to Hell; but because of their lack of knowledge of the truth, their punishment, according to Jesus, will be less than those who knowingly reject the truth. Think about the implications of what Jesus said. It will be better for the people of Sodom and Gomorrha than it will be for the people who grew up in church, in a culture with Judeo-Christian principles, who had a mom and dad that loved the Lord, who had preachers who taught them the Bible, and who were taught the right way but refused to use the key of knowledge by entering.

Peter expresses the same principle with what I call the "dogs and hogs" illustration. *"For it had been better for them not to have known the way of righteousness, than, after they have known it, to turn from the holy commandment delivered unto them. But it is happened unto them according to the true proverb, The dog is turned to his own vomit again; and the sow that was washed to her wallowing in the mire."* (2 Peter 2:21&22) If you have ever had a dog, then you know the truth of what Peter is saying. If you let it, a dog will go right back to eat its own vomit. That's a gross illustration, but it is a fitting one to display the folly of those who know the truth and have the key to change their lives but refuse to use it. They need repentance; but instead, they go back to the awful, disgusting mess of their sin. You can clean a hog, wash it up, and put a bow on it, but you cannot change its nature—once you let it out, it will go straight back to the mud. Pigs like mud. The mud is comforting and does not force them to change their ways. But it's still filth, even if it is comfortable filth.

Another negative impact of refusing to turn the key of knowledge to enter into the truth is that it destroys relationships with those who are in the truth. A hog does not care if you stink, but a person who wants to be clean and do right does not want anything to do with that mud. You cannot hug a hog without getting mud on yourself. That is why Paul told Timothy to "turn away" (2 Timothy 3:5) from those who refuse the truth. Why? The simple answer is because they are going to be a bad influence upon you. Second Timothy 3:6 says, *"For of this sort are they which creep into houses and lead captive silly women laden with sins, led away with divers lusts."* I heard a sermon once that warned people to watch out for the "creeps." You had better be on guard, because following those who refuse the truth leads to captivity. Here's the danger—those who are in captivity try to take others with them. They know they are not right, and they know they are not using the key; but rather than working for their freedom, they encourage others to join them. If you spend much time with those who are unrepentant of their sins, then you are on the road to snares. Turn away. If you are not in a snare today, do not rest content with just coming to church and learning more about God. Be sure that you are responding to the truths you learn by using the key. Take what you are learning and apply it, or you will find yourself in a snare.

When I was in New Jersey at a Reformers Unanimous meeting, I heard a wonderful testimony from a man who had been a champion boxer. He was a giant of a man. Now, I am not small; but when I shook hands with him, and his hand enveloped mine, I felt small. At one point, this man was on top of the world. He had been saved when he was young and for a time had grown spiritually. Then, he took up boxing. He was really good at it, but he said that the better he got at boxing, the more proud he became. He enjoyed the attention and the applause and the feeling that every eye was on him. He was the best, so he thought he did not need God. He did not turn the key; soon he was ensnared. He went all the way to the top of the boxing world; but then, he lost his crown in a fight with Mike Tyson, and everything came crashing down. He spiraled all the way to the bottom, ensnared by Satan. Then, he said he saw a sign outside of a church that said "Addiction Program." He turned the key, went inside, and started his journey back to freedom.

This man got in trouble because he knew what was right but did not do it. The answer is in the Bible. Instead of just getting to know what the Bible has to say, we need to apply it to our lives. That is what true biblical repentance is. It is not just something that's used once in an individual's life at the moment of salvation. There are frequent times when God reveals the truth to us through His Word. At that point, we have a decision to make. Now that you know the truth, what are you going to do about it? I urge you to take the key and use it to unlock the door to your freedom and your future.

CHAPTER EIGHTEEN

THE MEANING OF RECOVERY

"And the servant of the Lord must not strive; but be gentle unto all men, apt to teach, patient, In meekness instructing those that oppose themselves; if God peradventure will give them repentance to the acknowledging of the truth; And that they may recover themselves out of the snare of the devil, who are taken captive by him at his will." (2 Timothy 2:24-26)

I love the story of Jesus crossing the Sea of Galilee with His disciples in a boat. During the night, He was sleeping when a torrential storm came up. The disciples did everything they could to save the boat (remember that many of them were professional fishermen who know what to do during storms), and nothing worked. In despair for their lives, they woke Jesus and begged for help. He spoke to the wind and the sea and a perfect calm returned immediately. They reached shore in the land of the Gadarenes. What happened next is a perfect illustration of what it means to be recovered out of the snare of the devil. There was a man living in the graveyard who possessed by many demons. He was completely out of control.

He could not control himself, and he could not be controlled by others. Even when they bound him with chains, he burst free. He cut himself repeatedly and refused to wear any clothes. As a result of his behavior, he was driven out of society. Then, Jesus came! By the end of the day, that man was clothed, in his right mind, and sitting at the feet of the Lord Jesus. That is biblical recovery.

Jesus came not only to die and be raised again for our salvation, but also to recover those held in captivity by Satan. When Jesus began His public ministry after He had been baptized by John the Baptist in the Jordan River, He went back to the synagogue where He had worshiped growing up. That Sabbath day, He read these words from the prophet Isaiah, *"The Spirit of the Lord GOD is upon me; because the LORD hath anointed me to preach good tidings unto the meek; he hath sent me to bind up the brokenhearted, to proclaim liberty to the captives, and the opening of the prison to them that are bound."* (Isaiah 61:1) Jesus highlighted this prophecy because it was a description of His ministry. Today, His ministry is our ministry. We are meant to carry on His work of proclaiming liberty to the captives and helping recover them from the snares of Satan. Every Christian should be part of this work in dependence on God. Remember, as we have already seen, no one recovers without God. You and I do not simply decide to do the right thing; we only do that in response to God doing a work of repentance in our heart.

I want to call your attention now to the fact that everyone who is in the snare of the devil and has been taken captive by him has a personal responsibility for their freedom. They have no one to blame but themselves. It is the will of God that we be free from Satan's strongholds, and that we live our lives victorious in Jesus Christ. That is His plan, but achieving it requires that we must cooperate with God. If we have been ensnared, we must cooperate with the servants of the Lord who come to help us before we can recover ourselves out of the snares of the devil. With that said, we must answer this question: What does it mean to recover? The primary means of discovering the meaning of a biblical term is the Bible itself. So, let's look at some places where the Scriptures talk about recovery in order to gain God's perspective on the meaning. It is interesting, in light of our focus on spiritual warfare, to find that it is used in a military context in the Word of God. In First Samuel chapter 30, we see David at a low ebb in his life. He was running from Saul, and he and the men who followed him lived in a city called Ziklag. While they were away fighting, the Amalekites showed up and took away David's wives, his family, and all his fortune, as well as the families and belongings of all the men who were serving with him. When David and his men returned from battle and found out what had happened, they were both discouraged and angry. In fact, David's soldiers even discussed stoning him. David did what we should always do when we are under attack; he sought counsel from the Lord. First Samuel 30:8 says, *"And David enquired at the LORD, saying, Shall I pursue after this troop? shall I overtake them? And he answered him, Pursue: for thou shalt surely overtake them, and without fail recover all."*

What does recover mean? It means you get back what was taken away by the enemy. It is inevitable when we sin against God, sin against others, and sin against our own souls, that it will have a negative impact on our relationships. Part of the recovery process is a restoration of relationships. David and his men defeated the Amalekites and got their families back. A couple of years ago, a wonderful church in Buffalo, New York, decided to start Reformers Unanimous in their church. The pastor got the materials and being preaching and teaching the principles we use from the Word of God to his church. They decided to launch their program with a catered dinner for people from their community who are involved in law enforcement and the judiciary—those who spend a great deal of time working with addicted people. They invited me to come and speak. Before I spoke, a man gave his testimony. His addiction had broken all of his relationships. His parents had cut their ties with him. His wife had left him and taken their children. He had made a complete mess out of his life. They even had the detective who arrested him at the dinner! His parents were at that dinner. His wife was at that dinner. God had wonderfully restored those relationships. As he gave his testimony and thanked God for his recovery, he thanked the detective for being a servant of God! I saw a woman who is the warden over two large prisons sitting there with her mouth open in disbelief, marveling at his testimony. Recovery is more than stopping behavior we know is harmful, destructive, and sinful; it also includes a restoration of relationships that have been broken.

That restoration is not going to happen by accident. Someone came to me for help recently. This was not a stranger, it was someone I loved and had tried to help often before. Because of sinful disobedience, he was living in his car. When he asked for help, I said, "I want to help, but you will not let me be your pastor. You will not come to church. When I give you advice, you do the exact opposite. You cannot go to your family because you have burnt all those bridges; you deliberately and habitually sin. If I help you, what is going to change?" He got up and left. No matter how much you claim to want to be released from your snare, it is not going to happen by having someone else do it for you. You must repent and change before you recover. The devil will do everything he can to keep you from restoring and rebuilding your relationships. If he can destroy your relationship with your pastor, the members of your church, and the members of your family, then he has you in a vulnerable position.

David did not just recover his family, but he also recovered all of his position. I submit to you that recovery is also financially beneficial. Wherever you see biblical principles consistently applied, you will see economic benefit from it. You take the work ethic of the Bible as it is presented and you properly apply it, it will work. There are more than 2,000 Scripture verses that deal with the matter of finances. If you take those principles and apply them, then you will benefit. God does not promise you a mansion, a yacht, and a big fancy car; but He does promise to bless those who are diligent and faithful in handling their money. No one ever became a millionaire while making license plates in prison. While you are ensnared, your economic growth and economic stability is taken out of your control. But, when you are recovered, you can restore that economic stability once again. The cost of sin is enormous. The average cost of incarceration of an individual in a prison in our country exceeds $50,000 a year. If that person is not just free but recovered, he then becomes a taxpaying citizen rather than the tax burden to our country. Satan is a thief and a robber. When people are recovered from his snares, their ability to become prosperous grows exponentially.

Recover is also used in the Bible as a medical term. Second Kings 1:2 says, *"And Ahaziah fell down through a lattice in his upper chamber that was in Samaria, and was sick: and he sent messengers, and said unto them, Go, enquire of Baalzebub the god of Ekron whether I shall recover of this disease."* Ahaziah was the son of Ahab, one of the most wicked kings Israel ever had. He learned the wrong lessons from his father. When Ahaziah wanted to know whether he would get well after he was injured, he sent messengers to the priests of Baalzebub— the fly god of his enemies—to find out his prognosis. How foolish! In fact, God was so angry that he sent Elisha to intercept those messengers and tell them that the king would most certainly not get better. This is not rocket science. When you and I disobey God, there are physical consequences. When a person recovers and stops the behaviors that have been damaging their health, they are going to be better off physically. It is healthy to live for God and live life as God intended it to be lived.

David knew what it was like to suffer physical consequences for his sins. In one of his psalms of repentance he said, *"Hear my prayer, O LORD, and give ear unto my cry; hold not thy peace at my tears: for I am a stranger with thee, and a sojourner, as all my fathers were. O spare me, that I may recover strength, before I go hence, and be no more."* (Psalm 39:12&13)

David wanted to be able to recover his strength. He had reached the point where he could not go on. God was winning the battle, and David had no more strength to go on fighting Him. He needed to recover. What was going to happen when David recovered? His relationship with the Lord was going to be reinstated, but he was also going to regain his strength and physical vitality. Those who are ensnared by drugs and alcohol know this principle well. When they regain their spiritual freedom, their physical condition also changes for the better.

Let me give you one more Bible usage of recovery from the beginning of the public ministry of Jesus. We have talked before about His first sermon at Nazareth when he quoted the prophecy of Isaiah. Luke 4:18 says, *"The Spirit of the Lord is upon me, because he hath anointed me to preach the gospel to the poor; he hath sent me to heal the brokenhearted, to preach deliverance to the captives, and recovering of sight to the blind."* This statement was literally true, for Jesus healed a number of people who were blind. But, it is also a figurative declaration. When you are ensnared by Satan, your vision is clouded. You cannot see clearly what is going on. Often, I have heard people say, "How could I have been so blind?" When you are tangled in the snares, you do not realize your loss of clarity and vision. It is only later in looking back that you realize all the things you did not see while they were going on.

God's recovery is a full-scale recovery. It improves our relationships, our health, our finances, and our vision. In captivity, all of those things are lost or hampered. But then, things change. We come to the point where we say, "I'm going back to God. I'm going back to church. I'm going back to the Bible. I'm going back to hanging with servants of the Lord. God grant me repentance that I might recover myself out of the snare of the devil." So many times,

I have seen people who seemed to act like that demon-possessed man in the country of the Gadarenes. There is no greater joy than watching the transformation. First, they are running wild in the graveyards, untamable, cutting themselves, not dressed very well, screaming, and cursing. Then, you see them later on, fully clothed, sitting at the feet of Jesus, and in their right mind. That is recovery, and it is wonderful!

CHAPTER NINETEEN

THE BLESSINGS OF SOBRIETY

"And the servant of the Lord must not strive; but be gentle unto all men, apt to teach, patient, In meekness instructing those that oppose themselves; if God peradventure will give them repentance to the acknowledging of the truth; And that they may recover themselves out of the snare of the devil, who are taken captive by him at his will." (2 Timothy 2:24-26)

In order to avoid the snares of Satan, we need to understand how he places us in captivity and bondage. In Second Corinthians 2:11, Paul wrote, *"We are not ignorant of his devices."* One of the tools Satan is using effectively today is addiction, particularly to alcohol. Psalms 107:27 says, *"They reel to and fro, and stagger like a drunken man, and are at their wits' end."* I have never been drunk, but I have staggered. From time to time, over the years, our family has gone to Great America. Now, you have to understand that my idea of an amusement park is a place where I can read a good book. If I cannot do that, then I scout out all the food locations. I eat breakfast. Then, I find the people who sell elephant ears. Next, I head for the snow cone machines. I eat my way around the park. My wife and kids make fun of me for not wanting to go on the rides. They say to me, "You have got to come with us. We don't want an empty seat. Mom is going to be sitting with some strange man on Momo the Monster." That is always motivating to me, and I give in. I get on Momo, and he goes left and right; and my wife is screaming out of joy and sheer delight as we go upside-down and back and forth. When I get off, I stagger like a drunken man. I do not find that to be an enjoyable experience. Yet, many people are willing to go through that for the sake of drinking.

To understand what the Bible teaches about wine, you have to understand that the same word is used for both fermented and unfermented grape juice. When Christ performed a miracle at the wedding in Cana, He made good wine that was unfermented. The juice which we drink celebrating the Lord's supper is unfermented. It has not decayed. Why? Because it is a picture of the blood of Jesus Christ, and His perfect blood experienced no decay. His blood was pure of sin. It has become fashionable today to talk about drinking as an issue of Christian liberty. However, if you look seriously at the Word of God, it is not hard to see what God thinks about drinking. Proverbs 4:17 says, *"For they eat the bread of wickedness, and drink the wine of violence."* Is it any surprise to you that drinking alcoholic beverages is associated in the same sentence as violence? It is not a surprise to me. When people go out of their minds with drugs and alcohol, they are prone to do things that are destructive to others and often destructive to themselves. Violence and violent behavior are strongly associated with drunkenness.

Proverbs 20:1 says, *"Wine is a mocker, strong drink is raging: and whosoever is deceived thereby is not wise."* Here is an insight for you: if you are not wise, that makes you a fool. Wine makes people do things that are harmful and destructive.

Drinking also leads to poverty. Proverbs 21:17 says, *"He that loveth pleasure shall be a poor man: he that loveth wine and oil shall not be rich."* Proverbs 23:20&21 says, *"Be not among winebibbers; among riotous eaters of flesh: For the drunkard and the glutton shall come to poverty: and drowsiness shall clothe a man with rags."* Alcohol, illicit drugs, and mind altering or mood altering medications are the fast track to poverty. Proverbs 23:29 says, *"Who hath woe? who hath sorrow? who hath contentions? who hath babbling? who hath wounds without cause? who hath redness of eyes?"* Are those things that you really are anxious to get? I have never heard anyone say, "I hope I can get some woe today. Man I'm not sorrowful enough. I would like to get some trouble." Who has these bad results? Proverbs 23:30&31 tells us the answer: *"They that tarry long at the wine; they that go to seek mixed wine. Look not thou upon the wine when it is red, when it giveth his colour in the cup, when it moveth itself aright."* I have heard people say they think it is all right to drink in moderation. I guess they drink with their eyes closed! That's just stupid. It does not take even half a brain to figure that the whole tenor of the Bible is against the drinking of alcoholic beverages.

Before you think it cannot happen to you, consider this warning. Noah was a great man of faith, but he got drunk. Lot got drunk and laid in incest with his daughters, fathering the Ammonites and the Moabites, who for centuries have been enemies of the children of

God. Nabal got drunk. Amnon got drunk. There is not one positive example in the Bible of anyone doing anything good and beneficial by getting drunk—not one. Having said all that, we must understand that recovery is more than a call to stop drinking booze and abusing drugs. Recovery is a return to a proper state of mind, a regaining of one's senses. Our minds are important to God. There has never been a wicked society that was not the result of wicked thinking. In Genesis 6:5, we read, *"And GOD saw that the wickedness of man was great in the earth, and that every imagination of the thoughts of his heart was only evil continually."* If you want to be right with God and free from Satan's snares, your thoughts must be right. Much of the Sermon on the Mount deals with the subject of our thoughts. Matthew 6:27 says, *"Which of you by taking thought can add one cubit unto his stature?"* Mathew 6:28 says, *"And why take ye thought for raiment?"* Matthew 6:31 says, *"Therefore take no thought..."* Matthew 6:34 says, *"Take therefore no thought for the morrow..."* Why does Jesus spend so much time talking about our thinking? He does so because being sober is more than just not being drunk; it is right, controlled, and biblical thinking.

Second Corinthians 10:5 says, *"Casting down imaginations, and every high thing that exalteth itself against the knowledge of God, and bringing into captivity every thought to the obedience of Christ."* Satan aims for the mind. If he can control your thoughts, then he will be able to control your conduct. The devil would love to have you out drinking every night, but he will be just as happy if he can ensnare you with your own thoughts. A person who is not sober, is not thinking right, and will never be an effective witness to others.

When Paul was giving his testimony before Festus and Agrippa, his powerful words produced conviction in the heart of the Roman governor. Acts 26:24 says, *"And as he thus spake for himself, Festus said with a loud voice, Paul, thou art beside thyself; much learning doth make thee mad."* When you are free from snares and your thinking is right, your witnessing has power. Again it is not just drunkenness that clouds the mind; any habitual sin will ruin your ability to think clearly. It will captivate your thoughts and render you unable to focus on anything else.

Paul responded to the accusation of Festus. *"But he said, I am not mad, most noble Festus; but speak forth the words of truth and soberness."* (Acts 26:25) One of the most important blessings of sobriety is the power it gives our witness. I know a man who once was brilliant. He was a member of the Phi Beta Kappa honor society at his university. This is a Christian man, not a heathen. But, he took so many drugs that today he cannot string together a coherent sentence. Any hope of being an effective witness he once had is gone. God's purpose for your life can only be achieved as your mind comes under His control. In Romans 12:2, Paul writes, *"And be not conformed to this world: but be ye transformed by the renewing of your mind."* God is interested in transforming us into the image of Jesus Christ, but that is not possible if our lives are controlled by natural thinking; our minds must be renewed. A sober mind is a mind that is capable of being renewed. The word transformed here is the same word for the metamorphosis that changes a caterpillar into a butterfly. If we are going to become like Jesus, then our minds but changed into something else. The renewing of our minds is a reference to a renovation. That cannot happen if we are not thinking clearly.

Peter highlights the importance of sober thinking to victory against the devil. First

Peter 5:8 says, *"Be sober, be vigilant; because your adversary the devil, as a roaring lion, walketh about, seeking whom he may devour."* If you knew there was a lion stalking you, it would be the focus of your thinking. The problem is that we forget about the devil; he does not forget about us. Be alert to danger, or you will be easy prey. I was fascinated when I studied this and found out that the old lions that roar are not actually the lions that take down the prey. The younger lions are set along the trail, and then the older lion roars. When the animals run away from the sound of the old lion, they run right into the trap, the snare that has been set for them. Once they are captured and taken down, the old lion, the king of the beasts, comes up, and devours his prey. If you are not serious about this matter of your thinking, if you are not a sober-minded Christian, then you will be easy prey for the devil.

We see the concept of sober thinking again in First Peter 1:13-16, *"Wherefore gird up the loins of your mind, be sober, and hope to the end for the grace that is to be brought unto you at the revelation of Jesus Christ; As obedient children, not fashioning yourselves according to the former lusts in your ignorance: But as he which hath called you is holy, so be ye holy in all manner of conversation; Because it is written, Be ye holy; for I am holy."* We do not use the term "gird up our loins" much anymore; but in Bible times, it was a common expression. The robes men wore were not conducive to running. If they needed to get somewhere in a hurry, they would tuck the robe into their belt; girding it up. Once they had done that, they were ready for action. Metaphorically, we need to do the same thing in regard to our thinking. We need to be sober and think clearly and quickly. Our world is moving at such a rapid pace that we cannot afford to be slow learners. If we want to guard our own freedom and help rescue those who are ensnared, then we need to protect our minds and be sober in our thinking.

Not long ago, I was at a birthday party for two of my grandkids. While I was there, I spent some time talking to a businessman who is in human resources. He has the responsibility to interview and hire workers for his company. We were talking about the kind of potential employees he is seeing, and he made an eye-opening statement. He said, "I'm not that old, but I'm absolutely amazed at the inability of young people to think. We hire them, but I wonder how they could ever get a high school diploma. How could they graduate from college when they cannot think about the simplest of things?" The devil is no friend of grace. He is clever at providing us with diversions. People who watch 25, 30, or 40 hours or more each week of other people's lives through movies and television programs are dulling their minds. Those who read trashy literature harm their thinking. Kids, and even adults, spend thousands of hours on video games. Some of them are evil because of their content, but even the ones that are appropriate can draw people into hours and hours of diversion with no purpose at all.

Far too many Christians cannot give a reason for the hope that lies within them because they are spending their lives learning things that have absolutely no eternal value. There are people in the world who are searching for the truth who are highly intelligent and well-educated. They will not simply believe what you and I say because, "Momma told me it was the truth." That's wonderful, but Momma may not always be right. "I believe the Bible is the Word of God." That is a wonderful thing, but why do you believe the Bible is the Word of God? "Well I don't know. The preacher said the Bible's the Word of God." That is not good enough. This is a real issue. When people recover themselves out of the snare of the devil, their mind starts to clear up. If they follow that up by getting into the Bible, with the help of the Spirit of God, they can make up for lost time and gird up the loins of their minds. They can move forward and make a positive eternal difference in the lives of other people. Stay sober, and you will find yourself effective at rescuing captives and avoid becoming one yourself.

CHAPTER TWENTY

THE SNARING OF A BISHOP

"And the servant of the Lord must not strive; but be gentle unto all men, apt to teach, patient, In meekness instructing those that oppose themselves; if God peradventure will give them repentance to the acknowledging of the truth; And that they may recover themselves out of the snare of the devil, who are taken captive by him at his will." (2 Timothy 2:24-26)

We had a problem with mice in our garage. Mice have a very interesting way of letting you know where they have been. They leave behind little presents for you to find. So, when I found out we had mice, I got some mousetraps. Now I do not know who figured out that mice like cheese; but supposedly, that is the food they crave. It is not like you can ask them to rate different foods on a scale of one to ten. The mousetraps I bought even have the bait holder shaped and colored to look like cheese. What I found was that our mice liked peanut butter instead. That drew them right in. The devil does the same thing to us. He finds out what kind of bait will appeal to us to draw us into his snare. I believe there is an active spiritual warfare taking place in the unseen realm. Just as there are angels assigned to watch over us (Matthew18:10), I believe Satan has demons assigned to tempt us to sin. They are experts in knowing exactly what bait will be most effective in tempting you to enter the snare. They know whether you are a "cheese" mouse or a "peanut butter" mouse. Jesus told Peter, *"Satan hath desired to have you."* (Luke 22:31) Make no mistake—he wants **you** too. Satan has many, many snares. He is very crafty and creative. Especially, if you are in a position of spiritual leadership and influence, he would love to bring you down.

"This is a true saying, If a man desire the office of a bishop, he desireth a good work. A bishop then must be blameless, the husband of one wife, vigilant, sober, of good behavior, given to hospitality, apt to teach; Not given to wine, no striker, not greedy of filthy lucre; but patient, not a brawler, not covetous; One that ruleth well his own house, having his children in subjection with all gravity; (For if a man know not how to rule his own house, how shall he take care of the church of God?) Not a novice, lest being lifted up with pride he fall into the condemnation of the devil. Moreover he must have a good report of them which are without; lest he fall into reproach and the snare of the devil." (1 Timothy 3:1-7) This passage identifies for us the bait that Satan uses to snare leaders. Paul specifically talks about pastors—bishops—here, but this principle applies to all people who have a spiritual leadership responsibility. The word means one who oversees. It is a management word. If you are a parent, an employer, a teacher, or a pastor, then God expects you to have a spiritual purpose in your conduct.

There is one particular type of bait that the devil uses to snare leaders. He takes the same things that make us effective and uses them against us. In fact, the more successful we are in serving the Lord, the more vulnerable we become to this particular snare. Paul talks about those who "desire" to be leaders. These are good people with noble intentions, great motives, and sincere desires. What brings them down? It is pride that brings them down. Success increases our vulnerability to the snare of pride. We are warned so many times in Scripture not to take for ourselves the credit that belongs to God and others. We are told to walk in humility before the Lord. Proverbs 6:16&17 says, *"These six things doth the LORD hate: yea, seven are an abomination unto him: A proud look…"* At the very top of the list of sins that stink in the nostrils of Almighty God is pride. He warns us against pride and its devastating consequences over and over again.

Proverbs 11:2 says, *"When pride cometh, then cometh shame."*

Proverbs 13:10 says, *"Only by pride cometh contention."*

Proverbs 16:18 says, *"Pride goeth before destruction, and an haughty spirit before a fall."*

Proverbs 29:23 says, *"A man's pride shall bring him low."*

Perhaps, one of the best examples of the destruction brought by pride in all of Scripture is the story of Nebuchadnezzar. The prestigious king of the great Babylonian empire was forewarned by God through Daniel not to take the credit that belongs to God unto himself. He didn't heed the warning. One day Nebuchadnezzar stood and looked at the land, his great city and said, *"Is this not great Babylon that I have built?"* (Daniel 4:30) After seven long years of living as an animal, losing his mind, going on all fours, grazing like a cow, and growing his hair long and matted, his senses returned to him. Nebuchadnezzar bathed and put back on his royal robes and returned to his throne. Then, he gave a testimony about what he had learned from his experience. The great king concluded with these words: *"Those that walk in pride he is able to abase."* (Daniel 4:37) Pride brought down one of the greatest rulers the world had ever seen. You are not exempt. If you allow your heart to be lifted up and take credit for all you have done, then God is able to bring you low. It is far better to avoid the snare of pride and walk humbly.

Pride not only brought Nebuchadnezzar low, but it was the root of Satan's fall as well. Lucifer was one of three archangels, along with Michael and Gabriel. All of the other angels followed one of those three. Yet, as we study the stories of Isaiah 14 and Ezekiel 28, we see what brought Satan down. Though the Bible does not tell us specifically, there are indications that each of the archangels was tasked with certain responsibilities. Gabriel appears as a messenger, and Michael appears as a warrior. I personally believe that Lucifer was in charge of the worship in Heaven. If that is the case, he was responsible for overseeing all the music of Heaven, all the praise and glory that went to Jehovah God for eons and eons and time without time in eternity past. Somewhere along the way, he looked in a mirror and said, "My goodness, you're pretty special aren't you?" He began to take credit that belonged to God; and because of that pride, he was brought low.

Today he uses that same weapon to destroy leaders and successful ministers. Satan wants to bring down those who are having a positive effect and influence on the lives of others. Effective leaders are particularly vulnerable to pride because of their success. The devil knows that if he smites the shepherd, the sheep will be scattered. (Matthew 26:31) Notice how this snare works—the affected individual is "lifted up" with pride. If you have ever seen a hot air balloon, then you know what this expression means. The idea is to be lifted off the ground by being filled with hot air. Pride inflates our sense of who we are. Our head swells, and we get an exaggerated sense of our value. That is quickly followed by the fall. The word God uses here means to be "taken in" or "caught." We enjoy the taste of pride until the trap springs shut, and we find that we have been snared.

Then, we are told that pride brings us "into the condemnation of the devil." This is a legal term that refers to being charged with a crime. It is the concept we use today of being indicted. There are two applications to this truth. First, when we fall while trying to serve God and help others, we are falling to the same thing that brought down the devil. Second, through pride we open ourselves up to his attacks and accusations. The Bible calls him *"the accuser of our brethren."* (Revelation 12:10) He not only accuses us to God, but he uses our sins against us to bind us with the chains of guilt. He comes and whispers in our ear, "You're not so hot after all, are you big boy? You thought you were really something, but look at you now. Look at what you're doing. You claim to be a man of God and say you love the Lord, but then you did that." The worst part is that his voice resonates with us because we know he is right. We hear a voice in our heads that repeats over and over again, "Guilty, guilty, guilty." That condemnation is a terrible thing to face. Romans 5:8 says, *"There is therefore now no condemnation to them that are in Christ Jesus, who walk not after the flesh, but after the spirit."* It is wonderful not to be condemned, but Satan's snares lead us to walk after the flesh and to come into his condemnation. But, there is more.

Not only does pride bring condemnation, but it brings reproach as well. When others find out about our sin, there is shame. It is bad enough when we are the only one who knows about the problem, but it often does not stay that way. We are unmasked. Not only do we condemn ourselves, but others also look at us with judgment. The shame and embarrassment can be overwhelming. Listen to this carefully: God is not going to let it go. You cannot hide from Him. He does not think it is okay for you to continue to eat the devil's bait and stay in his snares. There is only one way out—you must humble yourself. James 4:6 tells us that God resists those who are proud but offers grace to those who are humble. That is the only way you can escape from the snare. There are two paths to humility—either you can humble yourself, or God can do it for you. I do not think you need me to tell you which one is the better choice.

We see this principle illustrated in the life of David. He was once a humble man after God's heart; but in time, his success and the blessings God showered on his life made him proud. He fell into the snare of thinking he deserved to have something that was not his and took Bathsheba, the wife of one of his inner circle of soldiers, the mighty men. Instead of repenting of his sin, he compounded it. David arranged for Uriah to be killed in battle, so that he could marry Bathsheba. He thought he had covered his tracks; and then Nathan showed up and said, "Thou art the man." David's sin became public knowledge. God inspired him to write what we know as Psalm 51—a song of confession and repentance. Since David refused to humble himself, God shamed him before the entire nation. Was that a bad experience? Absolutely, it was. But, it was better for David to be humiliated than for him to remain in the snare of Satan. The devil is out to get every believer, particularly those who are spiritual leaders. Watch out for the snare of pride. It may be attractive, but the ends thereof are the ways of death.

CHAPTER TWENTY-ONE

THE SNARE OF THE DESIRE TO BE RICH

"And the servant of the Lord must not strive; but be gentle unto all men, apt to teach, patient, In meekness instructing those that oppose themselves; if God peradventure will give them repentance to the acknowledging of the truth; And that they may recover themselves out of the snare of the devil, who are taken captive by him at his will." (2 Timothy 2:24-26)

There is another snare Satan uses very effectively to capture believers and render them ineffective in service to God, and that is a desire for riches. We see a warning about this snare in Paul's first epistle to Timothy. The Bible says, *"Let as many servants as are under the yoke count their own masters worthy of all honour, that the name of God and his doctrine be not blasphemed. And they that have believing masters, let them not despise them, because they are brethren; but rather do them service, because they are faithful and beloved, partakers of the benefit. These things teach and exhort. If any man teach otherwise, and consent not to wholesome words, even the words of our Lord Jesus Christ, and to the doctrine which is according to the godliness;*

he is proud, knowing nothing, but doting about questions and strifes and words, whereof cometh envy, strife, railings, evil surmising, perverse disputings of men of corrupt minds, and destitute of the truth, supposing that gain is godliness; from such withdraw thyself. But godliness with contentment is great gain. For we brought nothing into this world, and it is certain we can carry nothing out. And having food and raiment let us be therewith content. But they that will be rich fall into temptation and a snare, and into many foolish and hurtful lusts, which drown men in destruction and perdition. For the love of money is the root of all evil: which while some coveted after, they have erred from the faith, and pierced themselves through with many sorrows." (1 Timothy 6:1-10)

At first glance, you might assume that this is a criticism of wealth, but that is not true. Instead, these verses present a biblical and balanced view of wealth. Is prayer important to God? Of course it is. How about faith? Yes. Yet, if you take all of the verses in the Bible that talk about prayer or faith, that total is less than half of the number of verses that deal with money. It is an extremely important topic on God's agenda and on his mind. Money is important to us also. Satan knows that and uses it against us. To help you avoid the snare of the desire to be rich, I want to show you what it looks like to live with a biblical, God-directed view of possessions and an open hand and a willing heart to generously share what God has given to you with others. The distinction between living in freedom and being caught in a snare is not whether we possess wealth; it is whether wealth possesses us. The desire to be rich can snare a poor person with nothing, as easily as it can snare a billionaire—and perhaps, even more easily. It is all about what you desire the most.

The Bible is condemning or warning us that if we will to be rich, if we make as our goal and dream and life's achievement the accumulation of more and more and more for ourselves, then the Bible says we will fall into temptation and a snare. You see, people of every financial circumstance are prey to this bait of Satan, this desire that is fanned on every hand with advertising. But, it is a matter of desire, not a matter of how much one has. It is a desire to be rich. We see this distinction drawn vividly in the parable of the rich fool that Jesus told to warn of the danger of coveting possessions. *"And he spake a parable unto them, saying, The ground of a certain rich man brought forth plentifully and he thought within himself, saying, What shall I do, because I have no room where to bestow my fruits? And he said, This will I do, I will pull down my barns, and build greater; and there will I bestow all my fruits and my goods. And I will say to my soul, Soul, thou hast much goods laid up for many years; take thine ease, eat, drink, and be merry. But God said unto him, Thou fool, this night thy soul shall be required of thee: then whose shall those things be, which thou hast provided? So is he that layeth up treasure for himself, and is not rich toward God."* (Luke 12:16-21) A child of God may legitimately accumulate wealth if his purpose is not to accumulate for himself but so that he may give more for God and His glory and advancing the kingdom and the cause of Jesus Christ. That is what Jesus is talking about when He says "rich toward God."

We become rich toward God as we seek gain in order that we might give, that God might be glorified, and that His kingdom may be advanced. Paul gave Timothy instruction regarding his preaching to those who had possessions. *"Charge them that are rich in this world, that they be not highminded, nor trust in uncertain riches, but in the living God, who giveth us richly all things to enjoy; that they do good, that they be rich in good works, ready to distribute, willing to communicate; laying up in store for themselves a good foundation against the time to come, that they may lay hold on eternal life."* (1 Timothy 6:17-19) A Christian who is rich toward God views his or her giving as an investment in the souls of men and women and realizes that each gift is an investment laid up in the bank of Heaven. This is extremely important as a warning to us because our culture is so saturated with materialism, covetousness, and greed. And sadly, much of the false teaching about money actually comes from people who claim to be teaching the Bible. It is not a mistake that in First Timothy 6:3, that Paul, in the context of instruction regarding money, warned about false teaching. He said there would be some who "teach otherwise."

You will not have to look very hard to find a preacher who will tell you that it is God's will and plan for you to be filthy rich. Generally, they follow that teaching with one that says the key to enjoying this great wealth and luxury is to send them money first. Paul said that such teachers have the false idea that "gain is godliness." Increasing assets proves nothing about your relationship with God. In fact, the Bible says, *"The prosperity of fools shall destroy them."* (Proverbs 1:32) Riches are not always a blessing, and they are not an indicator of the condition of your heart. By contrast, riches are also not an indication of greed, dishonesty, and selfishness. Paul makes it plain that it is "the love of money," rather than money itself, that leads to all kinds of evil. Someone said you could choose between loving money and using people or loving people and using money. I think that sums it up pretty well. I thank God for the people in our church who are willing to invest their resources in helping reach people in need. Their bank accounts might not be very impressive to Bill Gates or Warren Buffett, but they are rich toward God.

The sin that leads us into the snare of the desire to be rich is the sin of covetousness. Coveting wants to have things and possessions for our own sake. Of course, covetousness applies to more than just material possessions; the Tenth Commandment lists your neighbor's wife, his servants, and his animals as objects that are off limits for your desire. If you love your neighbor as yourself, you will not want what belongs to him. Rather than being jealous or envious, you will rejoice at the blessings he has received. Money and possessions are amoral; they are neither good nor evil in and of themselves. But, when they fill our thoughts and our desires and lead us to focus on ourselves, then we have been ensnared by Satan. Because of our fallen natures, if our desire is to have more stuff, then we will never be satisfied. In his day, John D. Rockefeller was the richest man in the world. When he was asked how much it would take to make him content, he said, "A few dollars more." If money drives your life, then you will never have peace and rest.

Paul begins this warning by talking to servants who are "under the yoke." About one out of every four inhabitants of the Roman Empire in the first century was a slave. This yoke was not just metaphorical; many who heard this epistle in the church at Ephesus where Timothy was the pastor would have likely been slaves themselves. Some of them had masters who were good and kind; others, no doubt, had masters who were harsh and cruel. As slaves, these people had no rights, no union, no vote, and no voice. Paul warned them about not only their work but also about their attitudes toward their masters. In our day, we are so focused on our rights that many would reject this advice, but Paul was more concerned about God's honor and His name—and we should be too. Why does Paul address slaves in a passage about the snare of desiring to be rich? The answer is because people who have nothing are just as vulnerable to that temptation as anyone else. We live in a culture that is characterized by class envy. Political leaders and others fan the flames of resentment and jealousy for their own advantage. We hear a lot about equality—everybody have the same things. That is not God's plan. God's plan is for us to be content with His provision for us. Instead, we think, "If I just had that toy or this luxury item, or a bigger paycheck, then I would have it made." A person who thinks that is already ensnared; he just does not know it yet.

Any time you are not content, you are vulnerable to the desire to be rich. Today, we have an entire industry of brilliant people working diligently to destroy your contentment. That is what advertising is all about. There are numerous programs on television that a Christian has no business watching; but in truth, the most damaging material on your TV is probably found in the commercials. They sell you Satan's lies in thirty second segments designed to catch your eyes and your attention and make you want something you do not have. There is nothing wrong with asking God for things you need. There is nothing wrong with asking God for things you want. There is something terribly wrong with not accepting His answer if it is "no." If you are short of food and clothes, you have a problem. I can tell you that this is not the biggest problem facing most of us. If it were, there would not be so much talk about diets and losing weight and dropping off bags full of clothes at Goodwill! We have enough to be content; instead, we are allowing our desires to catch us in Satan's snares.

Paul warns us that the desire to be rich brings about a "fall into temptation." Jesus taught His disciples to pray, "Lead us not into temptation." The closer we are to temptation, the more danger we are in. There are some things we should stay as far away from as possible. When we desire riches, then we are being led down a pathway that will lead to a snare. Notice also that this wrong desire leads to "many foolish and hurtful lusts." These are desires and cravings that are outside of God's will for our lives. There is an abundance of "stuff" out there in the world that we can desire, but all the promises of the devil are lies. There is no contentment to be found in those things even if we get them. Finally, we see the end of this process. Those who stay in the snare of the desire to be rich "drown...in destruction and perdition." If I asked you at the beginning of a day if you wanted to do something that would drown you at the end of the day, I doubt you would be interested. Yet, Satan successfully convinces people—even Christians who should know better—to follow him on the road to ruin.

This snare poses a special threat to young people today. If you grow up in a materialistic culture where money is worshipped as a god, then it is easy for that to become the goal of your life. Someone who desires to be rich is not going to find the call to a mission field very attractive. But, God does not call everyone to the mission field; He calls us to live for Him wherever we are. And, for those who are living for money, living for God poses a conflict. Many people err from the faith as a result of making money their pursuit. Diane and I both grew up in a youth group with hundreds of teenagers. Today, many of those young people are no longer in church. Why? Something caused them to err from the faith. It is sad to hear the stories of the tragedies they have experienced. Moral failures, heartaches, business collapses, and sorrows have marked their lives. That is no surprise because that is exactly what God said would happen. They have "pierced themselves through with many sorrows."

Having sounded the alarm about this snare, let me address those who have already fallen into it. How can you recover yourself from this entrapment of Satan? The first step is to focus on becoming godly. If you live your life focused on the things that matter to Him, then your heart will be set on the eternal rather than the temporal. Second, we are to make a conscious decision to be content. God is not about equality. If you remember the parable of the talents, one servant got one, another got five, and the third got ten. The question is not how much you have but what you do with what you have and your attitude toward it. Third, we must be humble. Paul told Timothy to warn the rich not to be "highminded." If God has given you a measure of success, then remember that it is due to Him, not to you. If you see a turtle sitting on a fencepost, it is a pretty safe assumption he did not get there by himself. Finally, we are told not to trust "uncertain riches." Money may offer a promise of security, but it is a false promise. During the stock market collapse in the summer of 2011, the richest man in the world lost over seven billion dollars in one day. The money you have today could easily be gone tomorrow. Do not trust in riches, but trust in God.

Another protection from the snare that will help you keep the right attitude toward riches is further revealed when Paul tells Timothy to instruct the rich to be "willing to communicate"—or, in other words, to give with a willing heart. I carry a picture of Benjamin Franklin in my wallet at all times. I do that so that I will be ready to distribute to those in need. Thirty years ago, I watched a godly Christian businessman in our church give people "green handshakes." He would walk over to talk to a visiting missionary or a staff member for a little while, and then he would shake their hand giving them a $50 bill. After I watched him do that for a while, I asked him about it one day. He said, "I keep a $50 bill in my wallet so that when God says, 'give' I'm ready." God blessed his business, and he had more resources than many people; but his money never had him. So, I got in the habit of carrying around some money. I want my attitude toward riches to be right. I want to be ready to help people who are in need. It helps to protect me from the snare of the desire to be rich.

Life is not about stuff. We come into the world with nothing, and we leave the same way. Someone once asked a lawyer who was handling an estate for a very wealthy man, "How much did he leave?" The lawyer replied, "He left it all." You cannot take it with you, but you can send it on ahead. Jesus said, "*Lay not up for yourselves treasures upon earth, where moth and rust doth corrupt, and where thieves break through and steal: But lay up for yourselves treasures in heaven, where neither moth nor rust doth corrupt, and where thieves do not break through nor steal: For where your treasure is, there will your heart be also.*" (Matthew 6:19-21) If you use what you have—whether it's large or small—for God's kingdom and for the sake of others, then you are both guarding your heart and preparing for eternity. We need to get our focus off of ourselves and onto using every ability, every opportunity, every talent, and every resource that God has given to us. As we use what we have for His glory and His kingdom, we protect ourselves from falling into the snare of desiring to be rich.

CHAPTER TWENTY-TWO

THE SNARE OF SERVING A LITTLE "G"OD (PART ONE)

"And the servant of the Lord must not strive; but be gentle unto all men, apt to teach, patient, In meekness instructing those that oppose themselves; if God peradventure will give them repentance to the acknowledging of the truth; And that they may recover themselves out of the snare of the devil, who are taken captive by him at his will." (2 Timothy 2:24-26)

As we take our tour through the various schemes and devices Satan uses to ensnare people, our next stop takes us to Mt. Sinai. It may seem strange to go to the very place where God gave the Law to Moses to find the devil at work, but he was there. When Moses led the children of Israel out of bondage in Egypt, they stopped at Mt. Sinai on their way to the Promised Land. It had been 400 years since they left the land during the famine in the time of Jacob and Joseph; and in that time, many tribes had grown and developed and cities had been built. All of these people who had invaded the land were heathen, they were idolaters, and they did not believe in Jehovah God. These were the inhabitants of the land where Israel was going, and God issued a stern and serious warning to His people about the danger they would face in having their faith weakened and being snared by the devil.

"Behold, I send an Angel before thee, to keep thee in the way, and to bring thee into the place which I have prepared. Beware of him, and obey his voice, provoke him not; for he will not pardon your transgression: for my name is in him. But if thou shalt indeed obey his voice, and do all that I speak; then I will be an enemy unto thine enemies, and an adversary unto thine adversaries. For mine Angel shall go before thee, and bring thee in unto the Amorites, and the Hittites, and the Perizzites, and the Canaanites, the Hivites, and the Jebusites: and I will cut them off. Thou shalt not bow down to their gods, nor serve them, nor do after their works; but thou shalt utterly overthrow them, and quite bread down their images. And ye shall serve the Lord your God, and he shall bless thy bread, and thy water; and I will take sickness away from the midst of thee. There shall nothing cast their young, nor be barren, in thy land: the number of thy days I will fulfil. I will send my fear before thee, and will destroy all the people to whom thou shalt come, and I will make all thine enemies turn their backs unto thee. And I will send hornets before thee, which shall drive out the Hivite, the Canaanite, and the Hittite, from before thee. I will not drive them out from before thee in one year; lest the land become desolate, and the beast of the field multiply against thee. By little and little I will drive them out from before thee, until thou be increased, and inherit the land. And I will set thy bounds from the Red sea even unto the sea of the Philistines, and from the desert unto the river: for I will deliver the inhabitants of the land into your hand; and thou shalt drive them out before thee. Thou shalt make no covenant

with them, nor with their gods. *They shall not dwell in thy land, lest they make thee sin against me: for if thou serve their gods, it will surely be a snare unto thee.*" (Exodus 23:20-33) One of the snares of the evil one is getting God's people to serve the little "g" gods.

There is only one true God, but there are gods who are worshipped by different groups of people. The children of Israel belonged to the Lord. The Lord demanded and commanded their respect and their worship and their service, and He deserved it. He knew what would happen when they got to the Promised Land and were exposed to the influence of evil religious belief systems. The threat they faced was the same one we face today. The devil keeps using the same tactics and snares because they keep working. It is a tragic waste of potential for one who belongs to God, has been redeemed by the blood of Christ, and is on his way to Heaven to leave serving God and begin serving some other god. Let me make this perfectly clear: every single person on the face of the earth serves something. The choice is not between serving and not serving; it is simply who you will worship and serve. The Israelites were headed to a land with literally hundreds of false gods. Each city had its own god or gods; and in many cases, each individual family had their own. Often, these were little idols only a few inches tall that would be kept in a place of honor within the home or in the city. Though they were small, these little gods were extremely dangerous. You and I are just as much in danger of idolatry today as the Israelites were then. So, let's look at this warning God gave the people and see what we need to be looking out for in terms of Satan's snares.

The great preacher of the past T. DeWitt Talmadge had a sermon he often preached called "The Insanity of Sinners." It was taken from the story of the Prodigal Son, but I think that title fits this situation perfectly. We have the one true God who is perfect in love and gracious to us far beyond what we deserve. He forgives our sins and offers us a place in Heaven through no effort or merit of our own. He hears our prayers and has all power to meet every need we have. It is crazy to leave that God behind to worship some other god who is not real, has no power, and offers no help to our lives. Yet, it happens every single day. Many sincere Christian people are getting snared by the devil with false gods. Often, without even realizing it, many are worshipping at the feet of popularity, at the feet of prosperity, and the feet of power and influence, and at the feet of sensuality, and calling it worship of God and service for God. What insanity! What a tragedy!

If we wish to avoid serving the false gods which surround us today, just as they surrounded the Israelites thousands of years ago, then we must first obey the voice of the Lord. God said He was sending an Angel to prepare the way before them, and that the people were to obey his voice. It is a wonderful blessing to have an angel going in front of you and clearing the path, but I have to ask this question: What good is it if there is an angel before us if we are not listening to and obeying and following that angel? If we do not stay in close contact with and listen to and obey the voice of the Lord, then we forfeit the blessings, we forfeit the protection, and we forfeit the benefit of remaining snare free in our lives. God uses different ways to speak to us. Circumstances can give us guidance toward His will. Nature teaches us principles by which we understand His design. The heavens declare God's glory. But, the primary means of

God's revelation is His Word. In it, we find His will and His way, through the working of the Holy Spirit who lives within us. None of that helps if we do not listen and heed His voice.

Another method by which God speaks to us is through leaders He has placed in our lives. God appointed Moses as His spokesman to the nation of Israel. God would speak to Moses, and then Moses would speak to the people. Over and over and over again, the voice of the Angel which was the voice of the Lord, was given to the people of God through a human instrument. It was given through the voice of Moses himself that the people heard from the Lord. The principle this passage is teaching is that God reveals His will through the voice of duly appointed authority and leadership. If a spiritual leader tells you something that contradicts the Scripture, then that is not God's voice, and you should not follow that advice. But, when a leader ministers truth to your life, you had better listen and obey. If you do not, then you are placing yourself in a dangerous position and walking into a snare of Satan. Unlike you and me, the Israelites did not have the written Word of God to confirm what Moses said. They had to take it on faith that he was accurately conveying what God had told him.

Every teaching today should be tested and confirmed by Scripture. God referred to His Angel—His messenger—as the source of His voice to the children of Israel. In the letters to the churches in Revelation, each one is addressed to the angel, the pastor of the church. The pastor is meant to be God's messenger to His church. But, not everyone who claims to be a messenger from God actually is. In fact, Second Corinthians 11:15, tells us that Satan *"is transformed into an angel of light."* Our society pictures Satan as an almost comic figure with a red suit, forked tail, and pitchfork. Older portrayals showed him with a frightening, evil, and grotesque appearance. However, when he shows up, he normally is in disguise. He presents himself as a messenger from God. You had better careful what voices you heed. Over the years of my ministry, I have seen a steady growth in spokesmen portraying themselves to be orthodox and according to the Word of God, but their teaching and preaching is contrary to the clear principles and teachings of the Bible. Unfortunately, there are many sincere but naïve people who are snared by the devil unwittingly. These are not bad people; they are good people who think they are doing the right thing. It is critical that you and I are true to the Word of God, and that those to whom we listen are rightly dividing the Word of truth for us. Many people are worshipping a false god while thinking they are worshipping the true God. The sad truth is that there are churches that claim to be Bible believing, Bible preaching churches that are practicing idolatry instead of worship. Little by little, they change their position until over time they are ensnared. The church I grew up in and was saved in was once a Gospel lighthouse. Thousands came to Christ through the work of that ministry. But, if you go there today, you would not hear the Good News. This change did not happen overnight. It was a slow and gradual process of listening to the wrong voices and making little changes that brought them to ruin.

There have been times in my own life when I have compromised and become an idolater. Inevitably, those were times when I was not right with people in authority over me. When I was not in proper relationship with my mom and dad, I was vulnerable to the deception and the snares of the devil. There was a short slice of my teenage years when I disrespected my pastor, the man of God, and was not interested in the things of God. It was during that period that Satan snared me with wicked music. If you are not right with those who are in authority over you, then you are in a position of great danger. When God said to the children of Israel, "Obey the voice of the angel," He was not going to be talking to them directly. He was going to be talking to them through a duly appointed leader. And He said, "You better listen, or you're going to get snared by idolatry."

Not only are we to obey His voice, but we also must serve God exclusively. Exodus 23:24&25 says, *"Thou shalt not bow down to their gods, nor serve them, nor do after their works: but thou shalt utterly overthrow them, and quite break down their images. And ye shall serve the Lord your God, and he shall bless thy bread, and thy water; and I will take sickness away from the midst of thee."* The concept of idolatry is not always easy for us to understand. We tend to think of idolatry as worshipping statues or lighting candles. But, there was a common thread among many of the idols found in Scripture that reveals a fascinating insight into idolatry. Do you remember the story of Aaron and the golden calf? While Moses was on Mt. Sinai receiving the law from God, the people grew discouraged. They thought Moses would not return, so they asked Aaron to make them an idol. *"And Aaron said unto them, Break off the golden earrings, which are in the ears of your wives, of your sons, and of your daughters, and bring them unto me."* (Exodus 32:2) Hundreds of years later, Gideon did the same thing. Judges 8:24 says, *"And Gideon said unto them, I would desire a request of you, that ye would give me every man the earrings of his prey. (For they had golden earrings, because they were Ishmaelites.)"* Gideon made an idol out of the spoils of the victory God gave him—specifically out of the golden earrings of the Midianites. We find it again in the story of Jacob returning to Bethel to meet with God. He told his family to give up their false gods. Genesis 35:4 says, *"And they gave unto Jacob all the strange gods which were in their hand and all their earrings which were in their ears; and Jacob hid them under the oak which was by Shechem."*

What is the connection between idols and earrings? An idol is the one who holds your hearing—the voice to which you listen. Whatever or whoever it is, the one who has your ear is the one you worship. This further magnifies the importance of discerning the voice of God's angel and listening to him rather than the voice of the idolaters. Not only were these idols made from earrings, but they also were made of gold—that which was highly valued. What we value is what we worship. God wants us to value Him above everything else. Jesus made the cost of following Him plain. *"So likewise, whosoever he be of you that forsaketh not all that he hath, he cannot be my disciple."* (Luke 14:33) God will not take second place to anyone or anything in your life. He wants your ear. He wants your value. Though we do not live in a culture that has widespread distribution of little statues, we are still in danger of idolatry. Too many Christians are falling into this snare for it to be ignored.

CHAPTER TWENTY-THREE

THE SNARE OF SERVING A LITTLE "G"OD (PART TWO)

"And the servant of the Lord must not strive; but be gentle unto all men, apt to teach, patient, In meekness instructing those that oppose themselves; if God peradventure will give them repentance to the acknowledging of the truth; And that they may recover themselves out of the snare of the devil, who are taken captive by him at his will." (2 Timothy 2:24-26)

Some years ago, we had a dedicated, faithful man in our church. He was active in the work, he loved his family and his preacher, and he was leading and encouraging others to do right. He worked in our AWANA club teaching children on Wednesday nights. One day, he was presented with an opportunity. By changing his schedule, he would be able to receive overtime pay. The problem was that he would no longer able to be in church on Sunday night or Wednesday night. This was not a situation where he needed the money to provide necessities for his family; it was extra money. The overtime was not required; it was voluntary on his part. He made the change. We found other people to take over his responsibilities and places of service. For a while, he kept coming on Sunday mornings. However, he was not serving God as he had once done, but he was making more money. After a little while, the devil sprang the trap. Today, that man is divorced, he has lost his family, and he is living with a woman to whom he is not married. He wants nothing to do with God or church. He is in the snare of the devil.

If the devil had come to him and said, "I want you to leave your wife and family. I want you to quit church. I want you to stop studying your Bible and teaching children. Then, I want you to live in adultery with another woman. I want you to turn your back on God and follow me instead." If the Devil had come like that, he would have refused the offer in a second. But, the devil is deceitful and crafty, and he tempted this man with an opportunity to make a little extra money. A small compromise at the beginning led to serious consequences in the end. The devil snared this man with god of money. Sadly, this is hardly an isolated event. Over and over, the devil has snared people to love and serve something else besides the King of Kings and Lord of Lords. It is a tragedy when someone who once served with us changes sides in the war, when they leave the front lines and stop serving Jesus Christ. It is a tragedy for their lives, for their families, and for the church. God commands us to serve Him and no other gods.

I know that some of the people who will read this book are enjoying the benefits and blessings of being a Christian without doing a single thing for God in return. Think about the enormous blessings that are yours—you will never go to Hell, you have the indwelling Spirit of God, you have the Scriptures to read and follow, and you have other believers to help and encourage you on your journey. Too many believers today are only takers. The work of Christ through the local church is not a spectator sport. God means for each of us to be involved in some way, using what He has given to us to further His kingdom. Here is the problem: as I've said before, everyone serves something. If you are not serving God, then you are opening yourself up to the snare of the devil to serve some other god. We have bought into the humanistic mindset that thinks serving God is doing Him a favor. What folly! We owe God everything. Paul said giving our lives to Him was a "reasonable service." (Romans 12:1)

God makes His expectations of His people serving Him quite clear. Deuteronomy 10:12 instructs us to *"Serve the Lord thy God with all thy heart and with all thy soul."* Psalm 2:11 says, *"Serve the Lord with fear."* Psalm 100:2 instructs, *"Serve the Lord with gladness."* Romans 12:11 says, *"Not slothful in business; fervent in spirit; serving the Lord."* I have seen so many people claim they did not have time to serve God, yet they spend hours and hours on frivolous things of no eternal significance. "Pastor, I just can't walk and go on a bus route or go in a neighborhood and distribute literature. I just can't do it. I've got sore feet." Yet, those same people will get up before dawn and go out and run two miles." Something is wrong with that. Somebody says, "Well you know, I just don't have time to study the Bible enough to teach a Sunday school class." Yet, they have plenty of time to watch ten, twelve, or fourteen hours of television and movies every week. These are people in the snare of Satan. They are serving other gods. It is a tragedy. Serving God for a lifetime is not easy. People quit all the time. But, the rewards of remaining faithful are wonderful. I have been privileged to be in His work for more than forty years, and I do not regret it one bit. I would rather serve God than any of the gods that Satan tempts me to follow.

Let me show you another way Satan snares believers into serving other Gods. God promised Moses that He would drive out the inhabitants of the land of Canaan. *"I will send my fear before thee, and will destroy all the people to whom thou shalt come, and I will make all thine enemies turn their backs unto thee. And I will send hornets before thee, which shall drive out the Hivite, the Canaanite, and the Hittite, from before thee. I will not drive them out from before thee in one year; lest the land become desolate, and the beast of the field multiply against thee. By little and little I will drive them out from before thee, until thou be increased, and inherit the land."* (Exodus 23:27-30) God's plan was not for His people to coexist with the Canaanites; it was for His people to drive them out completely. If you try to coexist with wrong thinking and wrong worship, it will corrupt you. God said He would drive them out. But, that is not the whole story. In fact, the very next verse, Exodus 23:31 says, *"And I will set thy bounds from the Red sea even unto the sea of the Philistines, and from the desert unto the river: for I will deliver the inhabitants of the land into your hand: and thou shalt drive them out."* That is a different matter all together. Here is the principle: the removal of evil from your life is a cooperative effect. It can only be done in cooperative partnership between you and God. He will faithfully do His part, but you must do your part as well.

I have mentioned before that when I was a teenager, I was snared by worldly music. I liked that music, but it dulled my desire and appetite for the things of God. From the time I was 14 until I was 16, I was hooked on rock and roll. At the time, my parents did not understand fully the danger it posed, so they let me listen to it. But, over time, as the Spirit of God worked in my heart, I came under heavy conviction about it. I knew what I was listening to was not right. I reached the point when I said to God, "I'm sorry for this. I want you to forgive me. Root it out of my life." You know what the Lord told me? He said, "Root it out yourself!" I did not hear God's voice, but I heard from His Spirit loud and clear. That was on a Saturday. I went home and got my records (this was a long time ago). I took them out to the driveway. I got in my 1962 Buick LeSabre and started driving back and forth over those records. Mr. Bertolino who lived next door came out and watched me for while. I think he was convinced I had lost my mind. When I had broken all those records up into little pieces, I dumped them into trash bags. I took them to church the next morning and gave them to the preacher. He dumped them into the trash. Now, who drove rock music out of my life? Was it God, or was it me? The answer is it was both. God drove out the music, but I was behind the wheel. If you are sitting back waiting for God to do all the work for you, you are in a dangerous place. You can try to justify it and say, "Oh, it's just a little part of my life. I'm doing okay." That maybe true for now, but you are going to be snared before long. The devil just wants a little piece of your life. Drive it out—you and God together.

Next, we see that Satan snares us when we step out of bounds. Exodus 23:31 says, "I will set thy bounds." God had a clearly defined set of boundaries in mind for the land of Israel. One border was the Red Sea and one was the Jordan River and one was the Mediterranean

Sea. The point is that God has specific boundaries. If you stay inside them, you will be fine. Many Christians I know are really worried about what is happening out in the world. I am not saying that there are not things that are of concern to God's children, or that we should not be involved as citizens of our nation. But, our primary focus and concern should be what is going on inside the boundaries God has set for us. If you cross those boundaries, then you are headed for trouble and a snare. The problem today is that if you try to protect the boundaries and the ancient landmarks, even Christians do not like you. We get called all kinds of names. I have heard North Love Baptist Church described as legalistic. Do you know what legalism is? A legalist is someone who believes in works for salvation. So, to say that somebody who believes in separation that's stronger than yours (and everyone believes in some kind of separation) is a legalist is a misuse of the term.

We do not do anything to get saved. Keeping rules does not give us favor with God or make Him like us better. Keeping rules—His rules from His book—keeps us safe. Our only goal with our standards is to make sure we are living inside the boundaries of God's Word. I understand that good people have differences about matters of preference. That is just fine with me. Not everyone has to arrive at the exact same solution about everything. But, all of us ought to be inside God's boundaries. I like baseball. Baseball is played on a field with lines, fences, and rules. I have never yet heard anybody say, "Baseball is just too legalistic. It would be better to make up your own rules as you go along." We accept the rules of baseball because they are necessary to the game; but too often, we rebel at the rules of the Bible. Let me say this plainly. Every time you step outside of God's boundaries in the name of freedom or grace or liberty, the devil laughs. If your spiritual ears were open, then you would hear the sound of the snare closing behind you. Stay inside the boundaries, and you will not get trapped.

Finally, God issues a warning about making compromises with the enemy. *"Thou shalt make no covenant with them, nor with their gods."* (Exodus 23:32) The world is constantly pushing us to make little sacrifices in order to be more acceptable and not be so "extreme." You belong to God alone, and you cannot make a covenant with any other god without breaking your covenant with Him. You cannot give one inch to the devil without suffering the consequences. He will not be satisfied with an inch. He'll be back, drawing you another inch, and then another, and then another. Before it is done, he will want everything. Satan does not play fair. He wants to steal your joy, bind your strength, destroy your effectiveness for God, and keep you in chains and snares for the rest of your life. If you make "small" compromises with him, then that is where you will end up.

I remember so vividly when I was sixteen hearing a man who preached on the importance of moral purity. This man had contracted syphilis from a prostitute during a time when he was backslidden. He preached from a wheelchair because his health had been destroyed by the diseased. When he said, "Live for God and be pure," I got that message loud and clear. He was a living illustration of his message. That night, two of my friends and I made a covenant with God to keep ourselves pure. About a year after that, all three of us had girls that we liked. Our parents were not big on dating, so we did not go out alone. The three of us sang together in church sometimes (they were hard up for special music). One night, we were singing right before the preacher was going to preach. In the middle of the song, one of my friends broke down crying and ran off the platform. My other friend and I didn't know what to do. We fumbled our way through the rest of the song and then went to find him. He was still crying. We asked, "What in the world is going on with you?" He said, "My girlfriend is pregnant. I've broken my vow, my covenant with God to be pure."

That was a failure that was the result of a few little compromises that added up over time, but what happened next was even worse. The families made the decision that rather than publicly confess the sin and repent and do right, they would quietly slip off. They quit coming to church. They did not face the consequences of their actions. That young man had surrendered his life to the Lord, but he has never served Him. It is a tragedy. Yes, he sinned and did wrong. But, if he had come to God in humility and repentance and seeking grace, he could have been forgiven and restored. Instead, he remained in the snare. I wonder how many people that he could have and should have reached for Christ. It is not just the sin. He compounded the problem by not being restored, getting right with God, and dealing with his sin the right way. I have seen God recover and restore people who have done far worse to effective ministry for Him. No matter what you have done, God can still use you in some way—if you repent and return to Him. It is better to stay out of the snares; but if you have been caught by Satan, get out of the snare. Isaiah 55:7 says, *"Let the wicked forsake his way, and the unrighteous man his thoughts: and let him return unto the LORD, and he will have mercy upon him; and to our God, for he will abundantly pardon."*

CHAPTER TWENTY-FOUR

THE SNARE OF GIDEON'S EPHOD

"And the servant of the Lord must not strive; but be gentle unto all men, apt to teach, patient, In meekness instructing those that oppose themselves; if God peradventure will give them repentance to the acknowledging of the truth; And that they may recover themselves out of the snare of the devil, who are taken captive by him at his will." (2 Timothy 2:24-26)

I find the story of Gideon fascinating. He was not a man of perfect faith or great courage, but he had enough faith to do what God said. We find his name listed among the heroes of faith in Hebrews 11. As a result of his obedience, Gideon delivered his people and won a great victory. With 300 men armed only with trumpets and lamps, Gideon defeated the Midianites who had invaded Israel. That's the good part of the story. But, this man who was used by God in such a great way fell into a snare of Satan—a snare so severe that it captured the entire nation. After the battle was over, Gideon did one thing that was right (refusing to become king over the people) and one thing that was very wrong (making an ephod). *"Then the men of*

Israel said unto Gideon, Rule thou over us, both thou, and thy son, and thy son's son also: for thou hast delivered us from the hand of Midian. And Gideon said unto them, I will not rule over you, neither shall my son rule over you: the LORD shall rule over you. And Gideon said unto them, I would desire a request of you, that ye would give me every man the earrings of his prey. (For they had golden earrings, because they were Ishmaelites.) And they answered, We will willingly give them. And they spread a garment, and did cast therein every man the earrings of his prey. And the weight of the golden earring that he requested was a thousand and seven hundred shekels of gold; beside ornaments, and collars, and purple raiment that was on the kings of Midian, and beside the chains that were about their camels' necks. And Gideon made an ephod thereof, and put it in his city, even in Ophrah: and all Israel went thither a whoring after it: which thing became a snare unto Gideon, and to his house." (Judges 8:22-27)

Gideon was a man who believed in God. In fact, the first thing he did when God directed him to deliver the people of Israel was to destroy the grove of trees and the altar to Baal that his own father had built. Yet, Gideon also created a substitute religion that drew in the entire nation of Israel. Apparently, the ephod that Gideon made was a copy of the priestly garment that God commanded Moses to make for Aaron in Exodus 28. Though the Bible does not go into detail in explaining his motives, I do not believe that Gideon intended to do something that would destroy his family and damage his nation. The ephod was a vest-like garment, designed by God and made by Jewish craftsmen in the days of Moses. It had two great stones sewn into the shoulders called the Urim and the Thummim. God used those stones to reveal His will to the people through a process that the Bible does not explain. The Ark of the Covenant and the high priest were at Shiloh in those days, and people went there to inquire of the Lord what they should do.

The word Urim means "light," and the word Thummim means "perfection." When we seek His light and walk in it, we will never go astray.

What Gideon did was to take the golden earrings of the Midianites and make an ephod.

We do not know if it looked exactly like the original ephod that the children of Israel would have seen if they went to the house of God at Shiloh to worship. We do know that it was a substitute. I think Gideon's thought process went something like this: "I want to make this ephod so that we no longer need to go to Shiloh worship God. We will be able to stay home and worship God here. We will still seek for light and perfection. We will still desire the right things, but we will not go about it the way that God originally designed. We are going to create our own way to seek light and to seek perfection." It is not very popular to say this today, but it is not enough to simply want to do good things. We must also do good things God's way. Gideon's action seems innocent, but it led to destruction.

There is a fascinating clue as to why Gideon may have made this idea hidden in the story of his battle with the Midianites. Remember that after God finished paring the army down, Gideon only had 300 men left. Their nighttime raid panicked the Midianites, and they were fleeing. At that point, Gideon sent out a call for help. Judges 7:24&25 says, *"And Gideon sent messengers throughout all mount Ephraim, saying, Come down against the Midianites, and take before them the waters unto Bethbarah and Jordan. Then all the men of Ephraim gathered themselves together, and took the waters unto Bethbarah and Jordan. And they took two princes of the Midianites, Oreb and Zeeb; and they slew Oreb upon the rock Oreb, and Zeeb they slew at the winepress of Zeeb, and pursued Midian, and brought the heads of Oreb and Zeeb to Gideon on the other side Jordan. And the men of Ephraim said unto him, Why hast thou served us thus, that thou calledst us not, when thou wentest to fight with the Midianites?"*

The men of Ephraim were not happy with Gideon because they were not involved in the beginning of the fight. They were offended and felt like they had been slighted. I am not sure that they had any reason to be offended, but they were. The Bible says, "They did chide with him sharply." Most of us know what it feels like to get chewed out for something when we don't think we deserve it. I know it is hard to believe; but from time to time, people get angry with me and say some pretty nasty things. That is what happened to Gideon. He received a vicious verbal assault from the men of Ephraim. Rather than responding in kind, Gideon wisely placated them. In Judges 8:2-3, we read, *"And he said unto them, What have I done now in comparison of you? Is not the gleaning of the grapes of Ephraim better than the vintage of Abiezer? God hath delivered into your hands the princes of Midian, Oreb and Zeeb: and what was I able to do in comparison of you?"* Gideon smooth talked them and bragged on them and calmed them down. He pointed out the impressive nature of their victories and stoked their pride a little. They calmed down and went back home happy. I do not know if the men of Ephraim ever thought about that confrontation again.

Gideon remembered it though, and here is why it matters. Shiloh, the place where the Ark and the ephod and the high priest were, was in Ephraim. We do not know for sure, but I think Gideon was offended by what he viewed as an unjustified attack by the men of Ephraim, and he did not want to go Shiloh and have to be reminded of it every year. I suspect making his own ephod seemed like a logical solution to Gideon, but it led him into a snare. You will never solve your problems by running away from them. It would be nice if no one ever offended us, no one ever said anything mean or unkind or untrue, and no one ever falsely accused us. However, in the real world, we are going to have to deal with those kinds of issues. So many times, I have heard people say something like, "If that's the way they're going to treat me in that church, I'm not going there anymore. I can worship God at home. I don't need it." You may find a substitute, but you will also find a snare. Gideon not only created a problem for himself, but his actions led to the ruin of his family as well.

I did not just get into the ministry recently. I have been at this a long time—more than forty years of ministry, and a lifetime of going to church. I have been in independent, fundamental, Bible-believing, Baptist churches that preached and taught the King James Version of the Bible and that had a pastor who was a servant of the Lord since I was born—in fact, for the whole nine months before I was born. I have been in this all of my life. I will tell you very candidly that there have been and always will be conflicts between Gideon and the people of Ephraim. When you set out to do right and serve God, you are setting yourself up to suffer attacks, to be wounded, and to have your feelings trampled. It comes with the territory. When that happens, you have to make a choice. Are you going to keep going and keep doing right, or are you going to listen to the voice of Satan that tempts you to say, "I've had enough of that. I'm going to take my toys and go home"?

I was driving through a southern town recently; and between the hotel and the church, I passed about twenty Baptist churches. You would think that would be enough to convert the whole town, but that is not the way it works. Here's what happens. Second Baptist used to be part of First Baptist; but some of the people did not like the new song leader, so they left. There was a group who thought Second Baptist was too legalistic, so they split off and started Grace Baptist. But, Grace Baptist did not focus on the cross enough for some, so they left and started Calvary Baptist. That church was not friendly enough, so Fellowship Baptist was born. The people there spent too much time talking to each other, and soon there was Bible Baptist. It goes on and on and on. That is not God's plan! Instead of a healthy and growing and vibrant church, too often we have a bunch of little splinter groups nursing their hurt feelings and looking for alternatives to doing things God's way. Do not fall into the snare of making your own ephod. Trust God for His light and His perfection. Do not allow the actions of others to take you away from His plan or His people. The decision to create your own ephod has severe generational consequences. You are not just falling into a snare yourself; you are setting the stage for disaster for your children. All but one of Gideon's sons was murdered by their own brother, Abimelech. The tragedy of the ephod reached far into the future, beyond Gideon's own life and destroyed his children.

Brother Cary Schmidt of Lancaster Baptist Church has a wonderful ministry to Christian young people. He recently shared a letter he had received from a young lady who is a student at a Christian college. It's long, but I want to share it with you, because it perfectly captures the impact our sins can have on our children. This young lady wrote: "Dear Pastor Schmidt, A few years ago, I read your books *Hook, Line, and Sinker*, *Discover Your Destiny*, and *Life Quest*. I found them to be extremely encouraging and instructive. These books showed me that not only do you have a real heart for young people, but you also understand us well. I'm writing to ask you to consider writing a book to our parents and to our youth workers. Let me explain: I am a junior at a well-known fundamental Christian college. I grew up in highly respected fundamental, independent Baptist churches. I went to excellent Christian schools. My father's been a Christian worker serving the Lord since before I was born. One would think that my testimony would go something like this…I was saved when I was about five. I dedicated my life to God, and I've been growing and serving him; and now I'm studying to serve him full time in Bible College. But Pastor Schmidt, that's not my story at all. I didn't get saved until I was 17; and since I was 12 years of age and now into college I've struggled with serious issues. And I found out when I came to this Christian college that I'm not the only good kid who is or has struggled with serious stuff.

We struggle with issues like eating disorders, depression, suicide, cutting, pornography, gender identity, homosexuality, drugs, drinking, immorality, the list could go on. We listen to wild music, we idolize pop culture heroes, and we watch dirty sitcoms. We have no discrimination in our entertainment, in our dress, or any other aspect of our lifestyle. Obviously, I'm generalizing our problems. You would not find that in every Christian young person from a conservative background. Praise God for that, that some of us do not struggle with perhaps any of these issues. But others do. My point is that the problems that are supposed to be bad kids' problems belong to us too. And unfortunately, our pastors, our parents, our churches, don't know that we struggle with these things, and they don't know what to do with us when they find out we do. Quite frankly, I believe that if you grabbled the average Christian school worker, teacher, or youth worker and asked them, 'What would you do if you found out that one of the kids you work with was a homosexual?' they wouldn't know what to say. My point is not simply that they don't know what we struggle with or how to deal with it. I think there is a pretty simple reason why good kids struggle with these such serious stuff and that there is a solution. At the risk of being blunt, I'm going to be blunt. For many of us, our parents did not spend time teaching us to love God. They put us in Sunday School, and they put us in a Christian school. They took us to church every time the doors were open, and they sent us to every youth activity. They made sure that we went to the accepted Christian colleges. They made us sing in the choir, help in the nursery, be ushers, and go soul winning. We even did our teen devotions. We prayed before every meal. They made sure we did everything right, and they made sure that we did it. But they forgot about our hearts. So, to many of us, Christianity has become a religion of externals. If you do all the right stuff, you're a good Christian. That's why some walk away from church and others stay in church, but they just fill a pew. It's because they're struggling with stuff that our parents have no idea we're struggling with because they hardly know us."

May that never be said by any of our children. No one can shield you from having your feelings hurt, from having someone sit in "your" pew or park in "your" space at church. No one can stop people from saying things about you. But, you don't have to get offended by them and quit. That road leads to disaster. Don't try to improve on God's plan or find a substitute for His light and His perfection. A lot of churches today are dropping the tried and true methods of the Bible for new ways to reach people. Some of them are succeeding in building big crowds, but they're not building strong Christians. Don't make your own ephod—stick to God's design. Don't abandon Shiloh. Keep going to the place where you have met with God.

Let me say this as well. Learn to resolve your conflicts. It's easier to run away, but it doesn't solve anything. People are bailing out on churches, not because the church has changed its doctrine or lowered its standards, but because their feelings are hurt. People are walking away from marriages because they aren't getting what they want. People who are quitters are setting a devastating pattern for their families. The famous football coach Bear Bryant told his players, "The first time you quit it's hard, but every time after that it becomes easier and easier." May God make us men and women who won't give in and won't give up. Don't settle for a substitute; stick to God's design. Do not allow the criticism and attacks of others to derail you. Keep on going for the Lord. Do not fall prey to becoming easily offended and running from here to there. It results in a terrible snare. Do not make an ephod. Keep going to Shiloh. It will save you and your family a lifetime of grief.

CHAPTER TWENTY-FIVE

THE SNARE OF BAD FRIENDS

"And the servant of the Lord must not strive; but be gentle unto all men, apt to teach, patient, In meekness instructing those that oppose themselves; if God peradventure will give them repentance to the acknowledging of the truth; And that they may recover themselves out of the snare of the devil, who are taken captive by him at his will." (2 Timothy 2:24-26)

We have been looking at some of the snares of Satan which he uses to entrap people and bring them into captivity. Though Satan has many devices, traps, snares, and bait to entice us; perhaps, the one that he uses most often and most effectively, is the snare of bad friendships. There is a great warning for us on this topic in the book of Proverbs. *"My son, if sinners entice thee, consent thou not. If they say, Come with us, let us lay wait for blood, let us lurk privily for the innocent without cause: Let us swallow them up alive as the grave; and whole, as those that go down into the pit: We shall find all precious substance, we shall fill our houses with spoil: Cast in thy lot among us; let us all have one purse: My son, walk not thou in the way with them; refrain thy foot from their path: For their feet run to evil, and make haste to shed blood. Surely in vain the net is spread in the sight of any bird. And they lay wait for their own blood; they lurk privily for their own lives. So are the ways of every one that is greedy of gain; which taketh away the life of the owners thereof."* (Proverbs 1:10-19)

One of the men on our church staff, Pastor Haese, is an expert in hunting turkeys. He has turkey decoys that look like pretty girl turkeys. He has a caller that makes a sound that makes the ears of the male turkeys perk up. He has camouflage clothes that cover him from head to foot. And he has got enough guns to start a small war. When Pastor Haese goes out to hunt turkeys, he is ready for action. He gets up early in the morning, way before daylight, and makes his way out into the field. When the turkeys show up, he is ready and waiting for them. I was sitting in the office the other day when I got a text message from him that had a picture of the latest turkey he had shot. He is successful because he disguises his intentions. When Satan tries to snare us, he does not do it out in the open. As Solomon said in this passage, it is not going to work if the bird can see the net. Often, Satan uses people who are part of our lives, even our friends, to lead us to destruction.

In Ephesians 6:11 Paul warns us to prepare for the attacks of the devil. He wrote, *"Put on the whole armour of God, that ye may be able to stand against the wiles of the devil."* The picture here is of the devil lying in wait, setting an ambush, plotting a way to capture the unwary child of God, and wrecking and ruining his life. I am not surprised that Solomon would have much to say then in the book of Proverbs on this matter of being snared. He saw firsthand the dilemma that his own father, David, faced over the years of his ministry as people betrayed him, even his beloved and closest friends. David was betrayed even by his own family members, who could not be trusted, because they had an agenda that would bring about the ruin of the king of Israel. The Psalms are filled with David's laments about those who were attacking him. Psalm 38:12 says, *"They also that seek after my life lay snares for me: and they that seek my hurt speak mischievous things, and imagine deceits all the day long."* Psalm 64:5 says, *"They encourage themselves in an evil matter, they commune of laying snares privily; they say, Who shall see them?"* Psalm 140:5 says, *"The proud have hid a snare for me, and cords; they have spread a net by the wayside; they have set gins for me. Selah."* Psalm 141:9&10 says, *"Keep me from the snare which they have laid for me, and the gins of the workers of iniquity. Let the wicked fall into their own nets, whilst that I withal escape."* Psalm 142:3 says, *"When my spirit was overwhelmed within me, then thou knewest my path. In the way wherein I walked have they privily laid a snare for me."*

David certainly had experience with Satan using friends to try to ensnare him. It was a problem he faced again and again. Solomon wrote the Proverbs by inspiration of the Holy Spirit, but much of it is material his father taught to him. I think David must have worked to prepare Solomon to be the king, warning him of the danger of false friends and the snares that they lay for the unwary. In the passage we looked at from the book of Proverbs, we see information concerning some specific characteristics of people of whom we need to be very cautious and careful. If you interact with these kinds of people without keeping your eyes wide open, then you are in grave danger of falling into a snare. When I was growing up, there was pretty much only one kind of friend—the kind you saw at school, at church, or in the neighborhood. Today, people have "friends" in cyberspace. These are people they may never have seen in person, yet they pour out their hearts to them. Many Christians are being destroyed by their attempts to please people who are not really their friends. I was reading recently about the attempted assassination of then President Ronald Reagan by John Hinckley Jr. in 1981. Hinckley attempted to kill President Reagan, not because of a disagreement with Reagan's conservative policies, but because he hoped that his action would draw the attention of actress Jodi Foster. Hinckley had been stalking Jodi Foster after seeing her in a movie. He did not have a relationship with her, but he wanted one; and it drove him to try to kill the president. Your friends, even your media friends and people you have never met, can have great power and influence over your life. With that said, what characteristics in our friends should place us on high alert to avoid falling into snares?

First, according to Proverbs 1:19, we need to beware those who are "greedy of gain." A materialistic friend is a danger to your spiritual freedom and well-being. Whenever you are in the presence of someone whose goal and focus in life is more on the accumulation of things – their focus is on something new, something better, something bigger, and more and more and more; someone who is never satisfied with what God has given to them; someone who does not know the joy of contentment that we are supposed to have in the will of God – that is a warning signal that this individual could be used by the devil to lay a trap for you. Let me tell you something about human nature—greed is contagious. A materialistic person who is focused on getting more stuff is already in the snare we looked at earlier of desiring to be rich. They will try to take you with them. Beware those who are greedy of gain.

Greed is subtle, because it is so much a part of the fabric of our society. Do you remember the show, "Who Wants to Be a Millionaire?" The implied answer is: everybody. We live in a culture where people find their value and their identity in their possessions and bank balances. It ought to look weird to us for someone to focus on things that will all be gone in a few years rather than on things that will last forever. Instead, we view that as normal. Imagine going to the bank and asking for a loan. The bank officer will want to know what you have for collateral. Suppose you say, "I have thirty-four buckets filled with asphalt." He will probably look at you like you're crazy and say, "That stuff isn't worth much. We use it to pave the streets." Now, picture going to God and saying to Him, "Look at this. I have all these piles of gold!" Will He be impressed? Beware of those friends who live for possessions. They will lead you into a snare.

Second, you need to beware any friends who do not have high moral standards. Solomon gives a gripping warning in Proverbs 7 of the effect of an immoral woman; what he called a "strange woman" after a young man. *"With her much fair speech she caused him to yield, with the flattering of her lips she forced him. He goeth after her straightway; as an ox goeth to the slaughter, or as a fool to the correction of the stocks; Till a dart strive through his liver; as a bird hasteth to the snare, and knoweth not that it is for his life. Hearken unto me now therefore, O ye children, and attend to the words of my mouth. Let not thine heart decline to her ways, go not astray in her paths. For she hath cast down many wounded: yea, many strong men have been slain by her. Her house is the way to hell, going down to the chambers of death."* (Proverbs 7:21-27) A friend who encourages you to watch something that you know you should not, who brags about immoral behavior, or who uses risqué language is placing you in danger of falling into a snare.

The change in what society and even Christians now accept when it comes to immorality is startling. We have a dear old saint in our church who gave a testimony that when he was saved many decades ago. One of his first thoughts was, "Now that I'm a Christian, I can no longer look at *Life* magazine." I believe that if you showed anyone today—I'm talking about people in good, conservative, fundamental, Bible-preaching Baptist churches—a copy of *Life* magazine from the 1940s, they would say, "What's wrong with that?" Our senses have been dulled by exposure to the point where we now accept without question what once would have been shocking. That is a very dangerous position to be in because it indicates we are oblivious to the snares the devil is placing in our path to catch us and entrap us.

Third, Solomon gives a warning about those with uncontrolled tempers. Proverbs 22:24&25 says, *"Make no friendship with an angry man; and with a furious man thou shalt not go: Lest thou learn his ways, and get a snare to thy soul."* We live in a violent culture. You may say, "I don't have any angry friends." But I would ask, "What about your entertainment choices? Are you feeding your mind with violent movies, violent television shows, violent video games and violent books?" The Word of God warns that you will learn their ways and fall into a snare. The devil is perfectly content to influence your behavior through entertainment "friends" instead of with in person friends. He is subtle and crafty, and he will use any means he can to draw you into a damaging friendship.

The devil knows that most of us would reject open and blatant temptation. Instead, he uses lures, snares, traps, and the wrong kinds of friendships and influences to draw us away from God. If he can influence you to spend time with people, either in person or through online relationships, media and entertainment, who will lead you astray, then he knows he has a winning plan. While the problem of these negatives influences has been around since the fall, in our present day and age, we are inundated with them. I am of the opinion that we are losing this war terribly. This failure to recognize the potential snare is behind the fact that so many people today who once loved God and lived for Him and served Him have been snared by Satan. Wake up! Look around and be on guard. We are walking in a war zone every day. Guard your friendships and the things that influence you—they hold the key to avoiding one of Satan's most effective snares.

CHAPTER TWENTY-SIX

THE SNARE OF THE FEAR OF MAN

"And the servant of the Lord must not strive; but be gentle unto all men, apt to teach, patient, In meekness instructing those that oppose themselves; if God peradventure will give them repentance to the acknowledging of the truth; And that they may recover themselves out of the snare of the devil, who are taken captive by him at his will." (2 Timothy 2:24-26)

As we continue our look at some of the most common and most effective snares the devil uses to entrap us, we come now to the one found in Proverbs 29:25. The Bible says, *"The fear of man bringeth a snare: but whoso putteth his trust in the Lord shall be safe."* We see this principle illustrated over and over again in Scripture. Abraham lied about Sarah being his wife because he was afraid. Years later, his son Isaac did the same thing with his wife, Rebekah. Aaron made a golden calf for the people to worship while Moses was on Mt. Sinai with God. Saul offered a sacrifice instead of waiting for Samuel because he was afraid he would lose control over the people. David, when he was running from Saul, went and lived with the Philistines—the bitterest enemies Israel had. No matter how bold or courageous these men were at different times in their lives, the fear of man caused them to fall into a snare and do wrong.

One of the best examples of this is found in the life of the great prophet Elijah. He was bold, fearless, and faithful. He declared that it would not rain; he declared the widow would have enough food to survive if she fed him first, and he called down fire from God out of Heaven while single-handedly facing 450 prophets of Baal. This is no ordinary man. This is a greatly used man of God whose life was marked by courage. Then, Elijah got word that Jezebel was out to get him. The wicked queen provoked fear in his heart that hundreds of false prophets had not, and Elijah fled for his life. He left behind his place of service to God and sat down under a juniper tree and begged God to kill him. Why? What happened? The fear of man (and woman) brings a snare. It stops you from doing what you should do and encourages you to do what you should not do. In the New Testament, we read of a fascinating encounter between Peter and Paul. Paul was upset when he found that Peter had been eating his meals with Gentiles, but when other Jews came from Jerusalem, Peter stopped. There was nothing wrong with eating with the Gentiles. In giving in to the racial prejudice of the Jews from Jerusalem because of his fear of what they might say about him, Peter not only was snared, but he blurred the lines of the gospel and brought disgrace and confusion to the church. So often, the fear of man is behind our lack of witnessing. Earlier, Peter had denied the Lord three times. Why? The fear of man brings a snare. Too often, we are ashamed of Christ and of the gospel. We are ashamed to live as Christians ought to live. We are ashamed to carry gospel tracts. We are ashamed to have a Bible on our desk in our place of business. We are ashamed. If it can happen to Peter and Elijah and David and Abraham, then it can happen to us.

I think of the instruction God gave to the prophet Jeremiah when He commissioned him to the ministry. Jeremiah 1:8 says, *"Be not afraid of their faces: for I am with thee to deliver thee, saith the Lord."* Now if you know anything about the story of Jeremiah, he had a tough go of it. God wanted him to deliver a message that the people did not want to hear. God told him right up front that he was not going to see vast numbers of people converted. He would never lead a huge mega-church. In fact, God told him that not only would the people fail to respond, but they would make faces at him! I have seen it happen where someone was preaching the truth of God's Word and people in the audience respond with scowling countenances. If that happens to you, do not let it stop you! Don't be afraid. So many churches today have trimmed their sails and compromised their message because they are afraid the attendance will drop. I would rather preach the truth just to my wife and family than to preach a watered down message to tens of thousands! The truth does not change just because people do not like; and God called us to be faithful, not successful. I like what one preacher said, "If the preaching rubs you the wrong way, turn around!" By the way, God had to come back later and remind Jeremiah of this truth. In Jeremiah 10:5, God said a second time, *"Be not afraid."* Even if you have been courageous for years, you still are in danger of falling into the snare of being afraid of men.

Paul got a similar instruction when he arrived at the city of Corinth. In Acts 18:9, God appeared to Paul in a vision and said, *"Be not afraid, but speak, and hold not thy peace."* Why did God need to tell Paul that? The great apostle was having a tough time. In Acts 16, he was beaten and thrown in jail in Philippi. In Acts 17, he was chased out of Thessalonica by a mob who then found out he had gone to Berea. They followed him and chased him out of that city as well. Then, he went to Athens and preached without seeing the kind of results he wanted. I think Paul was probably a little bit discouraged by the time he got to Corinth. From our standpoint, we would look at the story of his life and say Paul had good reason to be afraid of men, but God wanted him to continue to boldly witness and preach the gospel. Jesus is calling you and me today to speak up. It is not popular in our culture anymore to be a committed, conservative, Bible-believing Christian. That is no excuse to hold your tongue. Everyone you meet should know that Jesus has made a difference in your life.

The fear of man is a problem you should expect to have to deal with. Even people who have outgoing personalities, the kind who never meet a stranger, still often find it hard to witness. I remember vividly a time when our youth pastor took us to downtown Kalamazoo to go soul winning. He had taught us the plan of salvation and had us mark the verses in our New Testaments, so that we could share the gospel. We loaded up with tracts and headed into town. I was about thirteen years old. By that time, I already had a job; and I was used to talking to people. I am not shy or introverted; and normally, I had no problem striking up a conversation with people. But that night, I was sweating. When you sweat in Michigan in December, you know something is going on! The youth pastor sent us out two by two. I went to a street corner with Dave (now my brother-in-law), and we were supposed to pass out tracts and ask, "Do you know for sure that you would go to Heaven if you died today?" Oh, that was a hard night! I had never met any of those people before, and it was not likely that I would ever see them again; but the fear of man was very real to me that night.

I have been in the ministry for a long time now. It is easier for me than it once was, but there are still moments when I find myself grappling with the fear of man before I begin witnessing to someone. Expect this in your life. If you let it, the fear of man will silence your witness for Christ. God could write the plan of salvation in the sky. He could plant the gospel in people's minds. But instead, He has chosen to commission those of us who are His children to take that message to the world. The devil does not want people to get saved, so he places the fear of man before us as a snare. During my first semester of Bible College, one of the courses we were required to take was Personal Evangelism. We were required to witness to someone every week—I mean actually present the gospel, not just be silent witness. Well, I had learned the plan of salvation and had been sharing it with people since I was thirteen, so you would think it would have been easy. But, we had to turn in an activity report every Monday in class; and it was amazing how many times I got to Saturday night and realized I had not shared the gospel with anyone all week long. I would like to tell you I witnessed because I had a burden for souls; but mostly, it was because I did not want to face the teacher on Monday without having done it. I had to face the fear of man and overcome it in order to witness. I have to do exactly the same thing today. I was a on a plane not long ago and sat next to a man. As we began to talk, I asked him what he did. It turned out that he was in charge of all the North American operations for one of the largest companies in America. Then, he asked me what I did. I told him I was a Baptist preacher, but before I did I went through a brief mental struggle. The devil wants to snare me with the fear of men, and he wants to do the same to you.

So, what is the solution? How do we overcome the fear of man and escape from this snare? The answer is found in the same verse that warns us of the danger. Proverbs 29:25 says, *"The fear of man bringeth a snare: but whoso putteth his trust in the Lord shall be safe."* The antidote for fear is faith. I have found this true in my own life. The more I have faith in God, the less I feel the fear of man. When my faith decreases, then the fear of man increases. This is apparently a problem that Timothy dealt with as well. Paul wrote to him with counsel on this very matter. *"I thank God, whom I serve from my forefathers with pure conscience, that without ceasing I have remembrance of thee in my prayers night and day; greatly desiring to see thee, being mindful of thy tears, that I may be filled with joy; when I call to remembrance the unfeigned faith that is in thee, which dwelt first in thy grandmother Lois, and thy mother Eunice; and I am persuaded that in thee also. Wherefore I put thee in remembrance that thou stir up the fit of God, which is in thee by the putting on of my hands. For God..."* notice this, *"...hath not given us the spirit of fear; but of power, and of love, and of a sound mind. Be not thou therefore ashamed of the testimony of our Lord, nor of me his prisoner: but be thou partaker of the afflictions of the gospel according to the power of God."* (2 Timothy 1:3-8) In this passage, we see three essential ingredients, three gifts from God which allow us to overcome the fear of man.

Paul first mentions power. This is not talking about working out with weights but about the presence of the Holy Spirit of God in our lives. He is the source of our power. He overcomes our fear. He overcomes our shyness. He overcomes the snares of the devil. In my own strength, I am not able to overcome the evil one. I cannot be an effective witness apart from the power of God on my life. We looked earlier at the warning God gave to Paul in a vision when he arrived in Corinth to not be afraid. How did Paul respond? In First Corinthians 2:4, he wrote, *"And my speech and my preaching was not with enticing words of man's wisdom, but in demonstration of the Spirit and power."* If Paul needed God's Spirit to be effective, it stands to reason that we do as well. Often, our witness is weak or lacking because we are not relying upon the power of the Spirit of God in our lives to make us bold and vibrant and effective witnesses for Jesus Christ. Before Jesus returned to Heaven, He commissioned the disciples to take the gospel to the whole world. But, first He told them, *"Tarry ye in the city of Jerusalem, until ye be endued with power from on high."* (Luke 24:49) It is the Spirit of God who overcomes our fear and maximizes the impact of our witness.

Next, Paul talks about love. Love has the power to overcome fear. First John 4:18 says, *"Perfect love casteth out fear."* If we genuinely love people with the love of God, then it will motivate us to speak up and give them the Good News. Too many Christians today are like Jonah in the Old Testament. When God called Jonah to go to Nineveh and preach repentance, he did not want to go. Sometimes, people say that Jonah was afraid to go to Nineveh, but that is not the case. Jonah did not want to go to Nineveh and preach because he knew that if they repented, God would deliver them—and he did not want that to happen. He wanted God to destroy Nineveh, not save it! It's a wicked world out there. As we see evil growing and people doing things that would not even have been thought of a few years ago, let alone bragged about in public, and if our hearts are not filled with love, then we may find ourselves with Jonah, wishing God would just wipe them out.

But, He is *"not willing that any should perish."* (2 Peter 3:9) God loves "those people," the ones we think are not worth saving—or even witnessing to. Why are we surprised when people who do not know the truth of God or the love of God act like heathens? Rather than judging and condemning them, should we not pity them? Should we not have compassion on them? Should we not give them the gospel? I did not get saved because I was special or because I deserved it. I got saved only by the grace of God. If He had not saved me, then I would be just as wicked and evil as anyone else. Love for others motivates us to overcome the fear that keeps us from telling them the truth. An appreciation and recognition of God's love for us should motivate us to love others as well.

The final gift from God that helps overcome the spirit of fear is a sound mind. A sound mind comes from knowing the Word of God. In the context of witnessing, we often do not speak up because we are afraid that someone may ask a question, and we do not know how to answer. We are afraid we may get stumped. I have found that if I tell someone that "I don't know," it is not the end of the world. If someone asks a question you cannot answer, just say, "I don't know the answer to that. But what I do know is this, God loves you. God created you and wants you to spend eternity with Him in Heaven, but you cannot because we are all sinners. We all need a Savior, and Jesus died for our sins." What we do know is sufficient to answer others if we use it. If you wait until you understand everything in Scripture, then you will never witness to anyone.

Commit to learning all you can. Keep yourself under the preaching and teaching of the Word of God. Study the Word for yourself. Be a disciple of Jesus Christ. As you get to know God and fall in love with Him, He will help you to fall in love with people. As you yield in obedience to the Spirit of God, He will empty you of yourself, and He will fill you with Himself. He will change you like He did those men and women on the day of Pentecost. Our part is to learn all we can and use what we do know. As we pour ourselves into the Bible and get to know the answers, then the Holy Spirit will give us a soundness of mind that will take our fear and transform it into faith and boldness and witnessing for Jesus Christ. The fear of man is a snare that captures many of God's people; but through faith, we can receive power, love, and a sound mind to overcome it and live in freedom.

CHAPTER TWENTY-SEVEN

RECOVER YOURSELF

"And the servant of the Lord must not strive; but be gentle unto all men, apt to teach, patient, In meekness instructing those that oppose themselves; if God peradventure will give them repentance to the acknowledging of the truth; And that they may recover themselves out of the snare of the devil, who are taken captive by him at his will." (2 Timothy 2:24-26)

Many years ago when I was in my twenties, I was preaching for a church on the Upper Peninsula of Michigan. They had a prison ministry that worked in the maximum security penitentiary near the church. They asked me to speak to the men in prison. We went through all of the security processes involved in getting inside a maximum security facility. I left my pen behind and had to take off my watch. Before the service was going to start, we had a little time to spend with the inmates. They had plastic tables and chairs, and we sat and talked to some of the guys there. I was not experienced enough then to know there are some questions you should not ask, so I looked at the man sitting across from me and said, "Do you mind me asking you what you're in for?" The man looked at me and said, "I took the life of my grandmother." I swallowed hard, not quite sure what to say to that. Then, he went on and said, "But I'm no longer in prison." (It looked like a prison to me!) "These are the boundaries that God has for me. This is where God wants me to live for the rest of my natural life. But, I'm not in prison. I'm a free man." When the service started, I watched as he sang. I could see on his countenance and hear in his voice the sincerity of his faith.

Not all prisons have guards and bars and fences. Some people inside a jail are free; many on the outside are incarcerated. It is possible to be in the most restrictive and painful of circumstances and yet experience absolute freedom. It is also possible to have complete freedom of movement and be in bondage. Throughout this book, we have looked at what makes someone effective at helping people escape from Satan's snares, what some of those snares are, and how we can avoid them. Now, I want to focus on God's message to people who are in bondage to Satan. Paul talked to Timothy about what it takes to help people "recover themselves." If you are in a snare, then you have a responsibility not to just sit back and stay there. As we have seen as well, it takes God and the help of servants of God to get out of a snare. This passage teaches that we do not get out of snares on our own. But, it also teaches that we must be engaged in and dedicated to our own recovery.

I think of David walking out to face the giant Goliath. This Philistine from Gath had been defying the army of Israel and blaspheming the God of Heaven. Yet, despite that stream of threats and curses, no one in the army dared to go out and fight Goliath. David was utterly unqualified in the eyes of the world to take on a giant. He was too young to have joined the army with his older brothers. He had no military training. When he offered to go and face Goliath, Saul looked at him and said, "You're just a kid." David told Saul how he had killed a lion and a bear while tending his father's sheep. It is fascinating to me that he tells the story twice. First, he says, *"I went out after him and smote him, and delivered it [the lamb] out of his mouth: and when he arose against me, I caught him by his beard, and smote him, and slew him."* (1 Samuel 17:35) Then David says, *"The Lord…delivered me out of the paw of the lion, and out of the paw of the bear."* (1 Samuel 17:37) Earlier, we looked at God's instruction to the Israelites regarding driving out the Canaanites from the land of promise and saw both God and the people working together. We see the same thing here from David. Recovery requires active involvement from both you and God to be successful. We will never recover ourselves without His help; but ultimately, we are accountable and responsible for our own recovery.

When the Bible talks about recovery, the context talks about regaining possession of what has been lost or forfeited. Earlier, we looked at the story of David and his men who had their families and possessions stolen by the Amalekites while they were away in battle. Their wives and children were gone, their cattle were gone, their gold was gone—all of their possessions had been taken. David prayed and God told him to pursue after the Amalekites and God promised that he would "recover all." When we yield to sin, when we are caught in a snare of the devil, something has been lost. If we remain there, we may find that everything we once had has been lost. God is able to restore relationships that have been broken. David's men were so upset by the loss of their families and belongings that they were actually talking about stoning him. That sounds like a broken relationship to me! Recovery helps us regain respect and trust that may have been lost as a result of our actions. Recovery also restores family relationships. So many times, habitual snares and sins destroy family relationships. God can put them back together again. David also made a financial recovery. Habitual sins carry an enormous financial cost. I believe if everyone lived according to the Word of God, then we could pretty much eliminate our entire welfare system. When sin gets a grip on our lives, it inevitably puts us in prison and impacts us financially. In America today, there is a lot of talk about all of the costs of the various government programs. They are spending our country into bankruptcy, but the real problem is *not* a government problem. The fundamental problem of America is that we have turned our back on God's plan for society—the sanctity of marriage between a man and a woman, a work ethic, caring for the needs of others, and accountability. We need a revival of recovery today.

The word used in Second Timothy for recovery means "a return to sobriety." That is what the Bible teaches recovery does for us. Often, the best way to understand or define a word is by contrast. Second Corinthians 5:13 says, *"For whether we be beside ourselves, it is to God: or whether we be sober, it is for your cause."* What is the opposite of being sober or being recovered? It is being "beside ourselves". When you are in the snares of the devil, you are not in your right mind. No matter what snares are laid before us to tempt us, we are always snared in our thinking before we are snared in our actions. When the Bible says here that you and I can recover ourselves out of the snare of the devil, it is describing a return or restoration to sanity. If someone is using alcohol or drugs, we say they are under the influence. What we mean is that they are not in control—something else is. How many times have we fallen for one of Satan's snares only to later say, "I don't know why I did that. That was so dumb. I must have been out of my mind." If you allow Satan to control your thinking, then you are on the road to disaster.

Sobriety is used in the New Testament, not only in reference to sanity, but also in reference to service. In First Timothy 3:2, Paul wrote, *"A bishop then must be blameless, the husband of one wife, vigilant, sober..."* Satan loves nothing more than to snare a leader. He knows the fall of a spiritual leader will have a dramatic impact on the followers. The snares of Satan will keep you from effective service for Jesus Christ. I know some men who had powerful and effective ministries, who reached people with the gospel, who were outstanding speakers in the pulpit, but today are completely out of the ministry. It is a tragedy to lose your service because you lose your sobriety.

Another way this word is used in the New Testament is in reference to our sight. Titus 2:12&13 says, *"Teaching us that, denying ungodliness and worldly lusts, we should live soberly, righteously, and godly, in this present world; Looking for that blessed hope, and the glorious appearing of the great God and our Saviour Jesus Christ."* Recovery restores your vision. It helps you see clearly again. The devil is an expert at hiding his traps. He finds our blind spots and uses them against us. Notice also the explicit connection between having clear vision and looking for the Second Coming. Few truths do more to protect us from the enemy than the wonderful and glorious hope of the second coming. Do not lose sight of the fact that Jesus is one day going to return for us.

Finally, we see that recovery restores us to a position of safety. First Peter 5:8 says, *"Be sober, be vigilant; because your adversary the devil, as a roaring lion, walketh about, seeking whom he may devour."* We must never forget that the devil is out to get us. He would like nothing more than to ruin you and me, rendering our lives useless to the kingdom of God. When I think of the analogy the Bible uses here, I am reminded of the story of David Livingstone. Born in Scotland in 1813, he was a brilliant doctor. When he heard the great missionary Robert Moffat speak, his life was transformed. Moffat said, "I have sometimes seen in the morning sun the smoke of a thousand villages where no missionary has ever been." Livingstone later said those twenty words changed his life. David Livingstone had a passion to take the gospel to Africa. One day, he made contact with a village where the people were having trouble with lions killing their livestock. Since Livingstone had a gun, he offered to help with the lion hunt. When they found the lion, Livingstone shot it; but while he reloaded his gun, the lion attacked. It destroyed Livingstone's shoulder, leaving his left arm crippled for the rest of his life. Finally, the men were able to kill the lion. There is a lion after you today. Like a vicious beast, the devil wishes to destroy, defile, and defeat you. He wants to bring you into prison in your thoughts and ruin your service for Christ. He wants to drive you insane. He wants to fill you with fear and render you ineffective in serving Jesus Christ.

But, thanks be to God, we have a Savior who loves us, who died for our sins, and who rose again from the grave. His Holy Spirit gives us the power over sin that enables us to be victorious believers, so that we do not have to live our lives snared by the devil.

CHAPTER TWENTY-EIGHT

THE DEVIL

"And the servant of the Lord must not strive; but be gentle unto all men, apt to teach, patient, In meekness instructing those that oppose themselves; if God peradventure will give them repentance to the acknowledging of the truth; And that they may recover themselves out of the snare of the devil, who are taken captive by him at his will." (2 Timothy 2:24-26)

Our enemy was originally one of three archangels specially created by God as spirit beings of immense power, immense beauty, immense talent, and immense ability. We are not facing an easy foe. He sets traps for the unwary, rendering them ineffective in service for the Lord Jesus Christ. There are a number of names for Satan in the Bible, and they give us insight into his character and nature. He is called Abaddon and Apollyon, Beelzebub, Lucifer, and Satan. He is also referred to and described as a roaring lion, a dragon, the father of lies, a serpent, the prince and power of the air, and the ruler of the darkness of this world. He is the son of perdition, the tempter, and the wicked one. There are more than one hundred references in the Word of God to our enemy. In our society today the word devil is used for to describe many things. We have deviled eggs and deviled ham. We use the figure of speech, "Between the devil and the deep blue sea." There are sports teams like the Duke Blue Devils and cartoon characters like the Tasmanian Devil. There is even a vacuum cleaner brand called Red Devil. While the name devil has been diluted, it is a serious word, and God used it here for a reason.

Names in the Bible have meaning and often give us insights into the person. The Greek word for devil, *diablos*, means one who slanders or falsely accuses. This gives us an indication that one of his primary means of attack is through his words. We must never forget that we have a real enemy. He is not an allegorical figure or a figment of someone's imagination. The devil is alive and active in our world today. We find a description of his fall in the book of Revelation. *"And there was war in heaven: Michael and his angels fought against the dragon; and the dragon fought and his angels, And prevailed not; neither was their place found any more in heaven. And the great dragon was cast out, that old serpent, called the Devil, and Satan, which deceiveth the whole world: he was cast out into the earth, and his angels were cast out with him."* (Revelation 12:7-9) We see here that not only was Satan cast out of Heaven, but all of his angels as well. The devil is serious about his efforts to destroy the kingdom of God.

We see his skill with using words to deceive and ensnare people in the book of Genesis. The devil walked into a perfect world where everything was "very good" and convinced Adam and Eve that they needed something they did not have. That is not an easy thing to do.

They had a perfect, personal relationship with God and with each other. What else could you want? The devil is not omnipresent as God is; he can only be in one place at one time. But, he also has at his disposal one third of the angels God created who joined in his rebellion and were cast out of Heaven along with him. I do not think the devil himself is paying attention to me; but just as the Father in Heaven has assigned angels to watch over us, the devil sends demons to work against us. Though the Bible teaches that only lost people can be possessed by these demons, they can have a clear and negative impact on believers as well. We see this illustrated in the life of King Saul. When we first see him, Saul is a humble man selected by God to lead His people. Over time, he made bad choices and refused to obey God. God allowed an evil spirit, a demon, to attack him. First Samuel 14:16 says that the evil spirit "troubled him." Saul was agitated, unable to find peace, because of this demonic attack. He became angry and irritable, and turned on people who were loyal to him. He eventually tried to kill both his loyal servant David and his own son Jonathan.

Jesus often dealt with people who were possessed by demons. Matthew 4:24 says, *"And his fame went throughout all Syria and they brought unto him all sick people that were taken with divers diseases and touments and those which were possessed with devils, and those which were lunatic, and those that had the pasly; he healed them."* Matthew 8:16 says, *"When the even was come, they brought unto him many that were possessed with devils: and he cast out the spirits with his word, and healed al that were sick."* Matthew 8:28 says, *"And when he was come to the other side into the country of the Gergesenes, there met him two possessed with devils, coming out of the tomb, exceeding fierce, so that no man might pass by that way."* When the Bible talks about someone who is possessed, it is not the word for ownership, but rather the word for control. To give you an analogy, you would not be saying the demon owned the car; but rather, in the biblical sense, you would say that he drove it. These demons operate under the radar, unseen, and unnoticed. They are part of the devil's plan to snare you.

Demons are the only weapon Satan has at his disposal. He also has human ministers and servants as well. I am not talking about people who are part of the Church of Satan; I am talking about people who meet in churches and claim to be Christians. Second Corinthians 11:13-15 says, *"For such are false apostles, deceitful workers, transforming themselves into the apostles of Christ. And no marvel; for Satan himself is transformed into an angel of light. Therefore it is no great thing if his ministers also be transformed as the ministers of righteousness; whose end shall be according to their works."* The devil is delighted when people go to a false church and believe a false gospel. They are inoculated against the truth, because they are content with what they have and see no need of salvation. Jesus told a parable that perfectly illustrates this truth of a Pharisee and a publican who both went to pray. *"And he spake this parable unto certain which trusted in themselves that they were righteous, and despised others: Two men went up into the temple to pray; the one a Pharisee, and the other a publican. The Pharisee stood and prayed thus with himself, God, I thank thee, that I am not as other men are, extortioners, unjust, adulterers, or even as this publican. I fast twice in the week, I give tithes of all that I possess. And the publican, standing afar off, would not lift up so much as his eyes unto heaven, but smote upon his breast, saying, God be merciful to me a sinner. I tell you, this man went down to his house justified rather than the other: for every one that exalteth himself shall be abased; and he that humbleth himself shall be exalted."* (Luke 18:9-14) The Pharisee was very religious, but he was not justified.

The devil can even use other believers to try to ensnare you. Though he cannot possess and control you, if you are not wary and alert, he can influence you to have a negative impact on others. He did this with Peter, using him to actually oppose Jesus. *"From that time forth began Jesus to shew unto his disciples, how that he must go unto Jerusalem, and suffer many things of the elders and chief priests and scribes, and be killed, and be raised again the third day. Then Peter took him, and began to rebuke him, saying, Be it far from thee, Lord: this shall not be unto thee. But he turned, and said unto Peter, Get thee behind me, Satan: thou art an offence unto me: for thou savourest not the things that be of God, but those that be of men."* (Matthew 16:21-23) Jesus was explaining to the disciples God's plan for redemption, and Peter opposed Him. In fact, when the Bible says Peter "took him," it literally means he grabbed Jesus by the shoulders to force Him to listen. Jesus called Peter, Satan, because he was doing the work of the devil in opposing the Lord. Then, Jesus said Peter was "an offence" to Him. This word comes from the Greek word for a special kind of trap. Many people in that time used an apparatus that had a small sapling bent over with bait placed on it. When the animal came and tripped the snare, the sapling would spring back up and capture the animal. What Jesus was saying was that Peter had allowed Satan to use him in an attempt to ensnare the Lord. Peter spent three years walking with Jesus, hearing Him preach, and learning from Him. Yet, here is Peter acting as a voice for Satan. I want to be so careful that I am never used to lead others into a snare. I want to remain alert and on guard, so I am rescuing people from the devil, rather than doing his ungodly work.

CHAPTER TWENTY-NINE

THE DEVIL'S WILL

"And the servant of the Lord must not strive; but be gentle unto all men, apt to teach, patient, In meekness instructing those that oppose themselves; if God peradventure will give them repentance to the acknowledging of the truth; And that they may recover themselves out of the snare of the devil, who are taken captive by him at his will." (2 Timothy 2:24-26)

We often talk of God's will for our lives, which is wonderful and good; but it is also true that Satan has a will for our lives. He desires to take us captive and keep us in bondage and snares, so that we will not be able to do and enjoy God's will. These two wills are in constant conflict. God has a plan and purpose for our hours and days; so does the devil. The two wills and plans are mutually exclusive. It is not possible for anyone to fulfill both. Either you are living according to God's will or Satan's. Satan wants to take us captive because he knows that if he has our life, we are unable to accomplish God's purposes. I want to highlight the difference between God's will and Satan's will. In

Second Timothy 1:1, Paul said he was an apostle *"by the will of God."* Paul did not select the course and plan of his life, God did. God chose him to be an apostle. God has a specific will for your life, just as He did for Paul. The word for God's will that Paul uses here is the same word used for the devil's will. It means "choice, preference, wish, desire, or plan.

Paul had committed his life to following God's will and plan from the moment of his conversion on the road to Damascus. Acts 9:6 says, *"And he trembling and astonished said, Lord what wilt thou have me to do?"* From that moment on, Paul lived according to the will of someone else. He did not control his choices or his destiny; that was now in the hands of the Lord. I want you to notice that living according to God's will is not something that takes years and years of being saved. It is meant to start at the moment you get saved and continue on throughout the rest of your life. It is a tragedy that so many Christians refuse to fully surrender to God's plan and will for their lives. There are many in Satan's snares. And though much grief and trouble accompanies being snared, the greatest tragedy is not the things which we do; but rather, the things we do not do because of the snare reveal the greatest tragedy. Inactivity is not acceptable for a child of God. Jesus said, *"My Father worketh hitherto, and I work."* (John 5:17) You cannot be like Jesus; you cannot do God's will unless you work for Him.

Some believers fall into the trap of thinking that as long as they do not get drunk or commit adultery or rob banks, they are okay. That is not enough. You can stay far away from the "big" sins and still be just as trapped by Satan as the worst sinner in town. What are you doing with the hours, the days, the weeks, and the years of your life? What are you accomplishing for eternity? What are you doing to build His kingdom and work in His harvest? The devil does not care what you do or don't do, as long as you do not do the will of God. If you are in church every time the doors are open but never grow spiritually, then you are doing the devil's will. The fact that there are thousands of believers all over the country doing exactly that is proof of how crafty our enemy is in setting his snares. They are caught in a trap and do not even realize it. Paul got saved and went to work. Within days, he was preaching about Jesus in the Jewish synagogues in Damascus. It is important to grow in your faith and learn the Word. It is vital to be discipled and mature as a believer. But, that does not happen from sitting around; it happens as and while you work. When we see people saved, as happens nearly every week at our church, we do not just abandon them. We work to get them in church, make sure they have new friends, and teach them the principles and precepts of the Word of God. We put them in a discipleship class to help them grow in grace. It is a horrible thing that some churches go out and witness, but then they do not do anything for the new converts. It is like a mother giving birth and then abandoning her child. But, as the new converts go through that process, we should encourage them to get involved in the work of the Lord.

You may think that God will not care whether you work or not—that kind of thinking plays right into the devil's hands. Listen to this stern and passionate warning from the Savior. *"Then Peter said unto him, Lord. Speakest thou this parable unto us or even to all? And the Lord said, who then is that faithful and wise steward, whom his lord shall make ruler over his household to give them their portion of meat in due season? Blessed is that servant whom his lord when he cometh shall find so doing. Of a truth I say unto you, that he will make him ruler over all that he hath. But and if that servant say in his heart, My Lord delayeth his coming; and shall begin to beat the menservants and maidens, and to eat and drink, and to be drunken; The lord of that servant will come in a day when he looketh not for him, and at an hour when he is not aware, and will cut him in sunder and will appoint him his portion with the unbelievers. And that servant which knew his Lord's will, and prepared not himself, neither did according to his will, shall be beaten with many stripes. But he that knew not, and did commit things worthy of stripes, shall be beaten with few stripes. For unto whomsoever much is given, of him shall be much required: and to whom men have committed much, of him they will ask the more.*" (Luke 12:41-48) Listen to me carefully. You cannot lose your salvation. If you have been converted, your place in Heaven is secure. But, according to this parable, if you are a wicked and lazy professing believer who refuses to do the will of God, then you had better check your spiritual condition. I know I do not want my portion to be with the unbelievers. I do not want to be beaten with many stripes. I want to hear the words, "*Well done, good and faithful servant.*" (Matthew 25:21)

Jesus lived His entire life to do the will of His Father in Heaven. We see this principle again and again in Scripture. John 5:30 says, "*Jesus said I can of mine own self do nothing: as I hear, I judge: and my judgment is just; because I seek not mine own will, but the will of the Father which hath sent me.*" What a contrast for many of us; we seek our will rather than God's will. The fact that Jesus did not seek

His own will does not mean that He did not have a will. Do you remember His prayer in the Garden of Gethsemane? *"Nevertheless, not my will, but thine be done,"* He said. (Luke 22:42) Jesus was always surrendered to the will of His father. In John 4:34, we read, *"Jesus said unto them, my meat is to do the will of him that sent me and to finish his work.* Again, in John 6:38-40, we read, *"For I came down from heaven not to do mine own will but, the will of him that sent me. And this is the Father's will which hath sent me, that of all which he hath given me I should lose nothing, but should raise it up again at the last day. And this is the will of him that sent me, that every one which seeth the son, and believeth on him, may have everlasting life: and I will raise him up at the last day."* We are called to follow His example and walk in His steps; that means we are to do God's will just as He did.

Paul explained this truth so clearly to Timothy. Second Timothy 1:9 says that God has *"called us with an holy calling, not according to our works, but according to his own purpose and grace."* Paul viewed his service for God as a privilege and a high calling. I believe that the Bible teaches that before the world began God established a plan for the life of every human being. He chose the time and place where you would be born. Some of us were privileged to born in great places like Michigan, and others were not quite as blessed! Wherever and whenever you were born, that was God's plan for your life. Each of us has unchangeable features, different talents and abilities, and different personalities. Those are part of God's plan for our lives. They prepare and equip us for the work He has planned for us to do—to reach His "holy calling." Sometimes, we complain the most about the things God gave us to fulfill His purpose. Sometimes, those small things that we do not place much value on are vital to keeping us out the devil's will and in God's will.

I have had the same wristwatch for a number of years. On the back, it says that it is waterproof up to 200 meters. Well, I have never taken it that far underwater; but last year, I did wear it while snorkeling. I am not sure why I need a watch underwater; it's not like I was checking the time while I was watching the fish swim by. When I got out of the water, I noticed that the face on the watch was cloudy. There was water on the inside. I took it back to the watch place and showed it to the man. He said, "You shouldn't take that watch into the water." I said, "It says right on it that it is waterproof to 200 meters." He said, "When that watch was new it could do that. But there is a little gasket behind the face. Over time, the gasket develops little cracks. They are so small that you cannot even see them. The pressure of the water finds those small cracks, and the water gets inside." Now, if you had asked me to name the most important parts of that watch, I would not have named that gasket—I did not even know it was there. But, the watchmaker knew I needed that part. God knows what we need to do His will, and that is exactly what He has given to each of us. If you are playing your role and doing your part, then God's work moves forward; but if you are not, then you are caught in the devil's snare. Are you doing God's will today?

Paul gave Timothy an important reminder that each of us need to hear. The spirit of fear does not come from God. (2 Timothy 1:7) Timothy had been sent to be the pastor at Ephesus. This was a great church, but even great churches have problems. There were people teaching false doctrine, and the city was filled with idol-worshippers. Because Timothy was a relatively young man, some of the people in the church apparently looked down on him. Timothy needed to be encouraged and reminded to keep on doing God's will. Not only did Paul tell him not to be afraid, but he also told him not to be ashamed. (2 Timothy 1:8) We should never be embarrassed or reluctant to do God's will. There may be opposition and there may be persecution and there even may be affliction; keep on doing right anyway. Do not be ashamed of your holy calling and your eternal purpose even if the world or other Christians view you with disdain.

When the going got tough and Paul got thrown into prison, many who had once looked up to him and followed him turned away from him. (2 Timothy 2:15) Now, that is discouraging. If you have ever tried to help somebody unselfishly, sacrificially, and poured your heart into their lives, only for them to turn around and turn their back on you, then you know it hurts. If you had asked Phygellus and Hermogenes and others who turned away from Paul, I do not think they would have said they were doing the devil's will, but they were. When you are not doing the will of God, then you are doing the will of the devil. The issue is not what we are engaged in, but it is what we are not engaging in that allows him to get what he wants. When the devil has your life, you forfeit the blessings which accompany living in the will of God. There is nothing to compare with serving Christ with your life. Serving the Lord is no guarantee that you will never be discouraged or cast down. It does not mean that you will not suffer; in fact, it means you probably will. But, it is worth it all. Far better it is to suffer serving Christ than to live in the snares of the devil.

Paul concludes this passage to Timothy with a word of thanks to a special friend. Second Timothy 1:16 says, *"The Lord give mercy into the house of Onesiphorus; for he oft refreshed me, and was not ashamed of my chain; But, when he was in Rome, he sought me out very diligently, and found me."* Paul talked earlier about those who turned away from him; here was one man who sought him out to help him. As far as we know Onesiphorus never pastored a church. We do not even know if he ever preached a sermon. But, he did God's will. He encouraged and refreshed Paul when he was in prison. He did not just happen across Paul, he put in the time and effort to find where he was and get there. Sometimes, we make the mistake of thinking the will of God is just for preachers and missionaries. It is for every believer.

The will of God is making a salad or a meal for a funeral. It is sending a card to people who are going through a tough time or struggling. It is saying a kind word to encourage hurting and suffering people. It is doing the work God gives you, large or small, without hesitation or complaint. You may think what you are doing is small, but it is not to God. Jesus said that simply giving a cup of water in His name would bring a reward. (Mark 9:41) A simple word from you may be enough to keep someone from quitting and to keep someone from falling into the snare of the devil. God has you here for a reason and a purpose. The devil wants to stop you from doing it. Here is my question as we end this study: are you actively and purposefully doing God's will today? My prayer is that you are committed to doing God's will with your life. I pray that you are not content to live in Satan's snare, but rather you will join in the great work of recovering those he has captured. I pray that when your works are tried by fire at the Judgment Seat of Christ they will be gold, silver, and precious stones that pass the test. I pray that when you see our Savior face to face and when you look into His eyes and He asks, "What did you bring Me?" that you will have crowns to cast at His feet. Do not go empty handed. Do not get caught in Satan's snare and do his will. Do not forfeit the blessings that accompany doing the will of God!